American Copia

An Immigrant Epic

American Copia
An Immigrant Epic

by

Javier O. Huerta

Arte Público Press
Houston, Texas

American Copia is made possible through a grant from the City of Houston through the Houston Arts Alliance.

Recovering the past, creating the future

Arte Público Press
University of Houston
4902 Gulf Fwy, Bldg 19, Rm 100
Houston, Texas 77204-2004

Cover design by Bryan Dechter
Photo by Jack Davidson

Huerta, Javier O.
    American Copia: An Immigrant Epic / by Javier O. Huerta.
        p.   cm.
    Text in English or Spanish.
    ISBN 978-1-55885-748-3 (alk. paper)
        I. Title.
    PS3608.U34964A8 2012
    811'.6—dc23   2012003145
                                                          CIP

♾ The paper used in this publication meets the requirements of the American National Standard for Information Sciences—Permanence of Paper for Printed Library Materials, ANSI Z39.48-1984.

12 13 14 15 16 17 18   10 9 8 7 6 5 4 3 2 1

Contents

Form N-652
Preface | xi

"*Ubi panis ibi patria*, is the motto of all emigrants."

—De Crèvecoeur, "What Is an American?" (1782)

dedicado a la memoria de mi abuelita chole

Soledad Huerta (1926-2009)

The Immigration and Naturalization Service (INS) processes applications and determines eligibility of people who want to become naturalized United States citizens. As part of the naturalization process, an INS Officer will interview you to determine if you are eligible for naturalization. An individual who seeks naturalization must meet the following requirements: lawful admission for permanent residence, a minimum residency period, a minimum period of physical presence in the United States, demonstration of good moral character and attachment to the Constitution, an understanding of the English language and knowledge of the history and government of the United States. At the naturalization interview, the INS officer will:

Provide Professional, Efficient, and Courteous Service and explain the nature of the interview and the requirement that the interview be conducted under oath.

Allow an Attorney or Other Representative who has filed a Form G-28 with the INS to accompany you during the interview. In addition, if you are exempt from the English language requirements, you may bring an interpreter to the interview, or the INS may select an interpreter for you. If you have certain disabilities, a family member, or legal guardian may accompany you during the interview, at the discretion of the INS officer.

Test Your Understanding of English and Knowledge of the History and Government of the United States, and provide you with the test results. Your understanding of spoken English will be judged by your answers to questions normally asked during the interview. If necessary, the INS officer will repeat or reword questions until satisfied that you understand the questions or do not understand spoken English. If you do not pass the tests at the first naturalization interview, the INS will schedule a second interview for you to take the tests again. If you are exempt from any of these requirements, or if you present a certificate from an authorized testing entity stating you passed the test, the INS officer will not test you at the interview unless there is evidence of fraud.

Receive Your Oral or Documentary Evidence to support your claim to eligibility for naturalization. You must also answer all of the INS officer's questions during the interview that relate to your eligibility for naturalization.

If you have questions or comments regarding your interview, you may ask to speak with an INS supervisor. You may also mail questions or comments to the district director or officer-in-charge of the interview location, or to the INS Executive Secretariat, Attention: Customer Service Comments, 425 I Street, NW, Washington, DC 20536.

After your naturalization interview, the INS officer will fill out the information below which you may retain with your naturalization records.

- -

A# _90-891-109_

On _11-28-99_, you were interviewed by INS officer _STROUD_. The results of the evaluation of your understanding of English and knowledge of the history and government of the United States are:

☑ You passed the English language test.
☐ You failed to demonstrate the ability to _____ speak/_____ read/_____ write English.
☐ You are exempt from the English language requirement, or the requirement was waived.

☑ You passed the history and government test.
☐ You failed to demonstrate a knowledge of the history and government of the United States.
☐ The history and government requirement was waived.

If during the interview you failed to demonstrate an understanding of the English language or a knowledge of the history and government of the United States, you _____ will/_____ will not be scheduled for another interview to take the tests again. The INS will notify you later of the final decision on your application.

grant

Preface

Mi abuelita Chole became a U.S. citizen in her seventies, and her decision to naturalize actually influenced my own decision to apply for citizenship. She likes to recount her INS interview and has related it to me several times. She says that somehow she managed to answer the questions the INS agent posed about her family, her home back in Mexico and her health. She says that the INS agent helped her with some of the words, and that throughout the interview she clutched the rosary beads in her pocket. Then the agent asked her to write the following sentence in English: "I Love America." She guessed "I," and "America" is spelled the same in English as it is in Spanish. This left mi abuelita with "Love." Clutching the rosary beads and praying to la Virgencita she looked around for an answer and noticed on one of her fingers a silver ring that my father had bought more than twenty years ago. On the ring, a serpent slithers and bends to form the letters L.O.V.E. My grandmother attributes this to the infinite wisdom and benevolence of God. I believe my grandmother may have cheated.

"Today I'm going to the grocery store"—this is the sentence that I was given. Inspector Stroup handed me a slip of paper and asked me to write it down. (I know the name of the agent not because I remember it but because I have kept a form she signed saying that I had my passed my exam. Considering that I have a passport and a Naturalization Certificate I probably don't need to keep any of these other forms. But having lived the undocumented experience I have internalized the need to document my existence.) This requirement to prove proficiency in English as part of the naturalization process conflates citizenship and language. I was being tested not on my ability to speak and write English but on my love of nation, my love for America.

Being in the very awkward situation of proving that I belong in a country in which I had lived already for twenty years, I was rather offended by the simplicity of my sentence. I felt that in a way I had prepared my whole life, at least since the first day I arrived in the United States, for this interview. I arrived in 1981 in the midst of a legal battle between undocumented school children and the state of Texas. A Texas statute denied state funding to any school district that opened their doors to undocumented children. In the late 1970s lawsuits were filed on behalf of those children, and while the issue was undecided the Archdiocese of Galveston-Houston established a couple of alternative schools. My family enrolled me in one of these schools, Guadalupe Aztlan in Houston's North Side.

In 1982, the "undocumented student" case reached the U.S. Supreme Court in *Plyler v. Doe.* In a 5-to-4 vote the Supreme Court ruled that undocumented students were not to be punished for the actions of their parents and that undocumented immigrants were to be considered as "persons" and were therefore protected under the Fourteenth Amendment, which calls for equal treatment under the law. The Texas Statute was deemed to be unconstitutional. Furthermore, the case raised the question of education as a right. Justice Powell in his concurring opinion wrote that because of the importance this society places on education the failure to educate a certain group of people would result in the creation of an underclass. Undocumented children, he commented, should not "be left on the streets uneducated." In the fall of 1982 I entered Houston Independent School District and through bumps and bruises, misunderstandings and mispronunciations I learned to read and write and speak English.

By the time of my INS interview, I was an English major at the University of Houston. So I felt ready to pass any exam on or about the English language. And "Today I'm going to the grocery store" was my sentence?! I wanted to tell the INS agent that I could do things with the English language that she could never imagine. Instead I settled for showing her that the sentence scans as iambic pentameter.

u / u / u / u / u /
Today I'm going to the grocery store.

"One day," I told her, "I will write an epic starting with that line." Poor Inspector Stroup. You were just doing your job. Accept my apologies. My mistake was to think that I or anybody else could master this or any other language. I have since learned of the abundance of language, which is both a great resource for writers and a daunting challenge. I consider this piece an epic about going to the grocery store. I am simply attempting to explore the abundance of experience found in that one sentence.

American Copia

Today I'm going to the grocery store.

December 14, 2007, Javier Omar Huerta Gómez is going with María in their yellow '74 VW Bug to the *Safeway* on Grand Avenue in Oakland, California.

When I was young, my mother bought our groceries from *Fiesta*. She also bought our shoes and clothes there. Thinking back on it, I have always wanted to write a stand-up comedy routine to be performed in the voice of a Mexican Jeff Foxworthy: "If your mother ever bought your tennis shoes from the same aisle she got the tortillas, you might be a mojado." Kids at school made fun. They could always tell who the little wetbacks were.

Today I am going to the supermarket and buy what I need with my good looks.

Last January, María and I walk approximately a mile around Lake Merritt to get to the *Albertsons* on 18th and after buying our groceries call for a taxi, which takes up to an hour. We learn not to buy ice cream or popsicles.

Tonight I will open my refrigerator and utter those wonderful words by John Keats, "O generous food." You may not know this line because critics have reduced Keats to "the

Great Odes." Recommendation: Read his Robin Hood poems.

Whenever I go back to Houston, I make sure to go to *Fiesta* on the corner of Bellaire and Hillcroft to get some elote from the Elote Man in the parking lot. Then I enter the store, not to buy anything but to count the piñatas hanging from the ceiling. America, when will you be worthy of your twelve-million-and-one Sancho Panzas?

One morning before dawn, Huerta will walk with his wife to the 24-hour convenience store to buy some low-fat milk, and his biographers will mistakenly call this "romance."

After a month of depending on taxis, María and I realize that there are unofficial taxis that drive people around the lake for five dollars. A woman named Laura loads our groceries into her station wagon. By the time she drops us off on the other side of the lake, we learn of her past on the East Coast and of her future in Texas. She does not tell us what she happens to be doing in Oakland.

On Sundays, my mother always bought the *Houston Chronicle* for the coupons it carried. She put on her glasses and spent about two hours clipping. She needed my help reading the small print because she couldn't make it out no matter how much she squinted or how many times she adjusted her glasses, and she also needed my help translating the English words. She had a special pouch for them. Sundays always smelled like coupons.

One November night in El Paso, I went to the supermarket and ran into Benjamin Alire Saenz. You may not know who he is because Chicano poets remain, for the most part, unanthologized. He is my mentor and doesn't know that we call him "el cura." Recommendation: Read his essay "I want to write an American poem."

The best time to go to the grocery store is late on a Saturday night because everyone must be doing something else. The only problem is that the shelves have not been restocked. "We used to go dancing on Saturdays," says María. I grab her, and we move to a cumbia beat down the canned food aisle.

An Ethiopian woman delivers enjira every afternoon to the corner store. She brings them in a minivan and unloads them herself. They sell, well, like hotcakes.

Once, in Stafford, Texas, Paul and his brother Roy stole their mother's food stamps. We went to 7-Eleven and used up a month's worth of food stamps on junk food. The clerk should have known better. After a while I left. They stayed behind playing video games. After I had been home for about half an hour Roy and Paul's mother stormed into our apartment and startled my mother and me. She threatened to call the police. How in the world would she feed her daughters? The food stamps were all she had. I snitched and told her where Paul and Roy were. She called the police and had her sons arrested. My mother did not talk to me for a week. That was the first time I understood that even white people can be poor.

Today I will notice that the supermarket has fourteen aisles and will remember that a young poet I know told me she had written a *Safeway* sonnet. Not being able to recall the verses, I will regret not having paid attention. I will wonder whether I will encounter her red hair as I turn into the fourteenth aisle.

In the summer of 2006 María buys a red cart in Oakland's Chinatown. We are now able to walk around the lake to buy our groceries and carry them in our red cart. We realize that if we walk fast enough we are able to enjoy ice cream and popsicles again.

May 14, 2006, while I wait my turn at the checkout stand, *Albertsons'* TV informs me that the poet Stanley Kunitz has died at the age of 100.

One Wednesday evening in the Fall 07 semester, Matt, Ben and I go to *Andronicos* in North Berkeley to purchase some wine and beer for the meeting of the Victorian Reading Group at Ruth's. I suggest we should take dessert, but Ben says somebody else is already taking care of it. He is right. We have bonbons. They are good good. Recommendation: Read and scan Christina Rossetti's *Goblin Market*.

Days of 1984, my mother would buy frozen everything: fish, fries, chicken patties and pizzas. She bought these items because they were easy to make. At the time, she worked in the kitchen at *Luby's* Cafeteria during the day and in the evening worked in housekeeping at the Westin Galleria. I made dinners for my brother and me. It was easy: place the fish sticks on a baking sheet and take them out when they were golden. My mother did not know that these items were high in trans fats and sodium. America, when will you learn that you will find no sweeter fat that sticks to your own bones?

After a trip to *Super Wal-Mart*, I will write the following line in my notebook: "the nature of hunger in the age of hypermarkets." I will also make a note that the line is an alexandrine with an extrametrical weak syllable.

4

I learned early enough that there were two classes of people in Houston: those that shop at *Randall's* and those that shop at *Fiesta*.

In fall of 2006, María and I learn about the *Safeway* on Grand, which means we do not have to walk around the lake anymore. Good. The joggers were beginning to be annoyed with us. If we want to, we can even take the AC Transit #12 to the store. It is a new store but the same system. María makes the grocery list, and I, paper and pencil in hand, make sure we stay under budget.

When I lived alone on Telegraph near Alcatraz, I stopped going to the grocery store because my fellowship money ran out.

Today we're going to walk down to the bodega on the corner and buy some chips. María is learning Arabic from the clerk, Ahmad. So far she knows how to say, Hello, How are you, Thank you and Farewell. I want her to ask him how to say, "Today I'm going to the grocery store."

One day I will step into a real life *Piggly Wiggly*, and only then will I be able to write a truly American poem.

Saturday morning María and I are going to the *Grand Lake Farmer's Market*. We will laugh when we see the "impeach" stand next to the peach stand because it is clever. We will buy a bag of salad and be fascinated with the edible flowers. How is it that flowers can be so delicious to us? We decide that they are so because we are descended from dinosaurs.

When Hurricane Rita was on track to hit Houston, my family decided not to evacuate and went from hardware store to grocery store to all kinds of stores looking for supplies. All the shelves were empty. They managed to find some food and filled buckets with tap water. It was my first semester at Berkeley, and they kept me updated over the phone. They could not find any plywood. I thought they would be blown away. Then a neighbor found some plywood in the baseball park behind the apartment complex. My brother Tomás and José Luis boarded up the windows of my mother's apartment. They then boarded up Mari's apartment as well. Later Rita changed course.

Once upon a time, George Bush the First did not know the price of a gallon of milk.

In "Considerations for American Freireistas," Victor Villanueva, Jr. discusses how one of his students works as a grocery checker. While this student drives a BMW, the GSI Villanueva must steal a cart to get his groceries home. Huerta reads and presents on this article for his Teaching Methods class. He discovers *Pedagogy of the Oppressed* and becomes impassioned with Paulo Freire. His composition director notices his enthusiasm and advises him that one can practice liberatory pedagogy as long as one does not announce it too loudly. Wanting to emulate Villanueva—after all they already have that "bootstraps" thing in common—Huerta attempts to steal a grocery cart, but nowadays they have these smart carts. Those things lock up on you. Huerta does manage to grow out his hair and his beard. His biographers will mistakenly call this "commitment."

Today I'm going to the grocery store to buy a six-pack of V8. It is the first step in reconciling with my father.

The one thing I remember the most about the day I first arrived in Houston from Mexico is that my aunts were at the grocery store. I asked my grandmother where my Tía

Pera was. She said she had gone to *Fiesta*. I misunderstood and thought she had gone to a party. I remember also one time when my youngest brother Saul and his friends were watching music videos and "Fiesta" by R. Kelley came on. In the video R. Kelley is at a party, and he and all his entourage chant, "Fiesta, fiesta." Then one of my brother's friends said, "Hey fu, sería más tight if they sing, 'la michoacana, la michoacana.'" And we laughed. We started dancing and chanting "la michoacana." We could not stop laughing. It was a joke not meant for you.

If I Forget Thee, O *SuperTienda Ramos*.

The day of my book release, Alejandro and I went to *Longs* to buy beer and wine for the party. We also needed forks but could only find sporks. In the end we went with assorted cutlery. We made sure to get receipts so we could be reimbursed. It was a lovely party. Alejandro read. Marcelle introduced me. And all my friends bought my book. While at the store, however, I was unsure whether you would show up.

One day in the future, Reiko envisions, we will have to explain to our younger generations how we used to go to these places called "supermarkets" and exchange a piece of paper for our sustenance. That the world begins and ends at the grocery store is an absurdity that we can no longer afford.

Tonight María and I are going to shop for groceries online.

Whenever we go to Nuevo Laredo, Tamaulipas, we purchase our groceries either at *Abarrotes Angélica* or at *Soriana*. To give you an idea, *Abarrotes Angélica* would be like your neighborhood convenience store, and *Soriana* would be like your hypermarket, department store and supermarket in one. But it would be a mistake to talk of equivalence in relation to Mexico and the United States. America, who could ever equal Domitila?

While waiting for his family at the *Fiesta* on Main, Huerta enjoys a roasted elote when he notices the headlines of one of the local Houston-area Spanish newspapers. "Literato Mexicano Octavio Paz Ha Fallecido." The headline grabs Huerta's attention not because it announces the death of the Mexican Nobel Laureate—to tell the truth, he had never heard of Paz—but because the combination of "literato" and "mexicano" sounds so strange to him. A Mexican man of letters? Huerta's biographers will mistakenly describe this moment as an "epiphany." In the next two months he reads every book by Paz that can be found in the stacks at the University of Houston's Anderson library. Huerta will incorrectly conclude that Paz's prose is more poetic than his verse. At this time, he is not yet mature enough to comprehend Paz's poetry. One of his biographers will correctly claim that Huerta was never able to mature to the level of Paz.

My first week in El Paso, Nancy gave me a ride to the MFA party at Lex's house. We stopped at *Albertsons*. I had never been to a writers' party before and didn't know what writers like. Nancy also had no idea. We decided on steak and a bottle of merlot.

Today I will be annoyed by a woman ringing a holiday bell in front of the supermarket. She will clang it without rhythm. María will drop a couple of dollars into the red bucket anyway.

During my second year in El Paso, feeling nostalgic for my earlier years, I buy all my shirts at the supermarket, which means I have to wear many Hawaiian-style shirts and a whole lot of polyester.

Once, in Stafford, Texas, Chato and I were walking back to the Mojays from the convenient store, and he threw a large paper cup into the ditch. A police car sounded its siren, and we stopped. One officer stayed in the car while the other came over and got in Chato's face. He emphasized how littering was a serious offense. Chato laughed. I didn't want to get in trouble, so I told Chato to be quiet. The officer ordered Chato to go into the ditch and retrieve the cup. Chato said no. I jumped in the ditch and got the cup. The officer stared down at Chato. Chato stared back. "You better start acting more like your friend, hear me," the officer said and jumped back into the patrol car. As they drove away, Chato flipped them off. We started walking, and I tried to tell him that he shouldn't give cops any more reason to mess with us. "Give me the cup," he said. I told him not to worry about it and that I'll throw it away. He snatched the cup from my hand and tossed it into the ditch. We heard the siren. Both officers flew out of the car and apprehended Chato. They ordered me to go home. They forced Chato into the car. I ran home and informed his mother. She said that she couldn't keep bailing him out of trouble. I then told my mother and was punished for hanging out with Chato.

Sometime earlier this year, I went to the supermarket and tried to pay in the express lane. The clerk said that I was over the 15-item limit. She counted my yogurts as five items instead of one.

I wish that grocery stores and supermarkets would carry my book. They could shelve it next to the cereal because I want people to read my poems during breakfast. I could even give readings over in the produce section. I promise not to mention mangoes, pomegranates or artichokes.

Neighbors share their concerns that the new *Whole Foods* on Harrison and the new *Trader Joe's* on Lakeshore will cause rent increases.

When María and I visit my mother, she takes us to *H.E.B* to buy whatever we may need or want during our stay. We get diet cokes, water, ice cream and popsicles. We offer to pay. My mother will not have it. She pulls out money and coupons from her purse. Coupons have always smelled like Sundays.

December 14, 2007, María and I are going to the grocery store in our yellow VW Bug. When we load and unload our groceries people stare at us because la Bete—that is what we have named our car—has its trunk in the front. People think our car has broken down. Some even offer assistance.

Me das algo, te doy dinero, los dos vamos en el camino.

    Es un sistema

        económico

            completamente básico.

El comprador-vendedor existe por el tiempo que se necesita.

    No hay

        pasado

            ni futuro.

Esto suena como un punto de vista del mundo muy frío.

    Pero hay

        momentos

            en los que es apropiado.

Cuando voy a la tienda no quiero conversar con la cajera

    o que me

        pregunte

            acerca de mi vida.

Ayer por la tarde, en el quinto día del pánico, empecé.
Un poco deprimido no podía salir a la calle. Yo no tenía
ganas de leer más noticias. Intenté trabajar un ensayo
contra mi amiga Alegría y el navegar por las nubes.
Me senté en casa por mi cuenta hasta casi la medianoche.
Mientras tanto, mi mamá me llamó para decirme,
"Es cada vez más difícil estar fuera de cobertura".
Mi respuesta, "Voy a la tienda a comprar leche y cereal".
Hoy es un día nuevo y estoy decidido a hacerlo bueno.
Estoy preocupado por Alegría, mi amiga. Una vez más.

On ta Jorge?

This story begins, as all our stories do, in the candy aisle of a South Central supermarket. A young baby in a stroller gorges on chocolates. He is alone. Not too far from this store a car is driving home. The family inside feels as if they have forgotten something. "On ta Jorge?" This is not the first time this mother has asked this question nor would it be the last—

When he was only 25 days old, the family placed "el perdido" in the paws of a female coyote. The family having made its own way to the new country waited for the coyote and the infant to emerge from the darkness. A night passed and no howl. Another night passed and no howl. "On ta Jorge?" The mother feared that her boy may have been devoured by the coyote. So she uncrossed the border and returned to a spot in the old country where the coyote had recently been sighted. A night later the mother found the boy wide-eyed in the warm bosom of the female coyote, who having lost her way nursed the boy until he would be returned to his mother's arms—

And as the family turns their car around, hoping that the boy will be waiting for them in that South Central supermarket, they do not know that 6 years later they would go on a longer journey in search of the same boy—

An autobús makes its way from Guadalajara to Colima. Around 5 in the morning, the autobús makes a rest stop. El perdido and his father go to the restroom. The son feels that he is old enough to use the urinal all by himself, so the father allows

13

him. Few minutes later no one has seen Jorge. The family goes to the media and to the authorities for help. The family goes to a psychic, but the crystal ball does not know the answer to "On ta Jorge?" On the fourth day the mother enters a church to talk to the priest. "Padre, sé que hay magia negra porque hay maldad en este mundo. Pero si la magia negra existe entonces también tiene que existir la magia blanca. Le suplico que me ayude a encontrar a mi hijo." El padre instructs her to take la estampita del Santo Niño de Atocha and wrap it in a pair of her boy's socks. "Y en menos de una semana," el padre says with holy authority, "usted encontrará a su hijo precioso." To pay back the saint, her son would have to wear the gown of the Santo Niño de Atocha for a month and would have to make a pilgrimage to the saint's church in Plateros, Guanajuato. Three days later, the family found the boy in an orphanage in Michoacán—

"On ta Jorge?" The family rushes into the grocery store and runs up and down the aisles. The mother finds her querido perdido covered in chocolate.

Amapola: A Play

Characters:

NENE (Young Cashier)
MARIELA (Friend Cashier)
MAGDALENA (Slowest Cashier in the Grocery World)
ROSIE (Manager)
HECTOR (Bagger)
ANA (Security)
PRÍNCIPE AZUL (Customer)
THE STARE (Customer)

Scene I

A Small Mexican Grocery Store. 5 registers. 5 aisles. A long line of customers for the masa factory. NENE works the middle register. MARIELA works the far right register. MAGDALENA in slow motion works the far left register.

NENE: (*Over loudspeaker.*) Estimados clientes. Sin ustedes yo no tuviera chamba. Por eso les quiero dar las gracias . . .
ROSIE: (*Just her voice over loudspeaker.*) ¡Caramba!
MARIELA: Mírala. You like to be in trouble, Nene.

Enter ROSIE

ROSIE: Deja eso. ¿Quién te crees? This isn't *Alcanzar una Estrella.*

NENE: Oh, es que I thought you had left, Rosie.

ROSIE: And that would make it fine? ¡Póngase a trabajar!

ROSIE *exits*

MARIELA: Nunca aprendes, Nene. I wonder why she hasn't fired you.

NENE: (*Takes the price tag off one of the go-backs and puts it over her name tag.*) What are you talking about? Because she knows how valuable I am.

MARIELA: You do know that says, $1.99, right?

HECTOR *enters.*

HECTOR: I swear that masa line wraps around the block like three times.

NENE: Yeah, it gets longer every day.

HECTOR: Yeah, you could say that las masas quieren más masa.

NENE: I'm going to have to say, Eh. Not one of your best jokes.

MARIELA: I liked it, Hector. It was funny.

HECTOR: Thank you, Mariela. I'm going to go help Magdalena bag groceries.

MARIELA: Hector is crazy about you, Nene. ¿Por qué no le haces caso? He's tall, light and handsome. And sweet.

NENE: Ay no, he's too shy. And he's always telling me those corny jokes. And besides I'm meant to be with Príncipe Azul.

MARIELA: Oh, I forgot to tell you. Mr. Handsome came in yesterday morning.

NENE: What?! Man, he always comes in when I'm not working. But one day I'm going to ring him up.

ANA *enters.*

ANA: Nene, hay viene tu príncipe.

ANA *exits.* PRÍNCIPE AZUL *enters.*

MARIELA: Órale, I guess that day is today. You're right. He is
handsome enough to be in a telenovela.

NENE: I'm nervous. Talk to me about something else. Q'onda
con la Barbara?

MARIELA: Pos nada. Still not talking. Dice Hector que Bar-
bara dice que she's going to quit and go work at Super A. Tú
crees?

NENE: What?! She's going to our rival store. I can't believe
she'd do that. Traicionera. Amapola for life. (*Throws up an
A with her hands.*)

ANA *enters.*

ANA: Cuidado, Nene. Ahí viene The Stare.

NENE: Oh no. Bueno, gracias por el aviso, Ana.

ANA *exits.* THE STARE *enters.*

MARIELA: Have you told Rosie about that creep yet?

NENE: I complain about him all the time, pero Rosie no hace
nada. Because he's a customer not an employee.

THE STARE *walks past the registers staring at* NENE. *She
stares back.*

MARIELA: I hate the way he looks at you.

NENE: Me, too . . . Oye, you and Barbara should get back
together before she has to change sides and go to Super A.
You guys were the cutest couple in Amapola.

MARIELA: Don't think that's going to happen . . . Oooh, Qué
mala suerte! Your príncipe got in Magdalena's line.

NENE: Bueno, no tan mala because she's really slow, and at least now I can stare at him for a while.

MARIELA: La pobre Magdalena. Ya no puede. She gets slower every day.

NENE: Oh. I think he got tired of waiting in Magdalena's line. He's coming this way.

NENE *rings up the customer in front of* PRÍNCIPE AZUL

PRÍNCIPE AZUL: Buenas tardes. Un aguacate.

NENE: Buenas tardes, Señor. Un aguacate. 59 centavos.

PRÍNCIPE AZUL: Su nombre?

NENE: Por qué? Hay algo mal con su recibo?

PRÍNCIPE AZUL: No, I would just like to know your name.

NENE: Adilene

PRÍNCIPE AZUL: Adilene, you should take that price tag off. Then you could be priceless.

PRÍNCIPE AZUL *exits.*

MARIELA: Wow! Nene. "Priceless." Jaja. No mames.

NENE *is enjoying her moment when she looks back to see that* THE STARE *is in her line.*

THE STARE: (*Points to her price tag.*) Esa, también.

NENE: Perdón.

THE STARE: (*Points to her price tag.*) Dije eso que esta ahí.

NENE: No, solo es broma.

THE STARE: No, ¿cuánto vale?

NENE: Ya le dije que no está a la venta. Su total es $5.55.

THE STARE *pays. Exits.* NENE *shakes her head and takes off the price tag.*

Scene II

Aisle #3. Cereal and Tortillas. Music playing. Cumbia. NENE *dances with mop.*

ROSIE: (*Just her voice over the loudspeaker.*) Nene, póngase a trapear.

Music stops. NENE *knocks some cereal boxes over. She begins to reshelve the cereal boxes when* THE STARE *walks into the aisle and passes close behind her.*

THE STARE: (*Whispers into* NENE*'s ear.*) Te ves hermosa hasta parada ahí.

THE STARE *exits.* NENE *stays frozen in place.*

ROSIE: (*Just her voice over the loudspeaker.*) Nene, póngase a trabajar!

NENE *stays frozen in place.*

Scene III

Aisle #3. Cereal and Tortillas. NENE *is still frozen in place.* MARIELA, ROSIE, HECTOR *and* ANA *stand in a half-circle around her.* MAGDALENA *enters and through the duration of the scene walks in slow motion toward* NENE.

MARIELA: Eit, Nene!
ANA: Y qué le pasó?
ROSIE: No sé. Pero that guy that is always staring at her was here around the same time.
HECTOR: She looks so beautiful standing there.
MARIELA: (*Poking* NENE*'s arm.*) Can you hear us, Nene?

19

ANA: A ver tú, Rosie, regáñala. A ver si te hace caso.

ROSIE: Oye, muchacha, what do you think, that it's break time? Póngase a trabajar!

They wait. No movement from NENE.

MARIELA: Y tú, Hector. Dile unos de tus chistes.

HECTOR: Es que she doesn't like my jokes.

ROSIE: Just try it anyway.

HECTOR: Hey, Nene, what does the corn tortilla say to the wheat tortilla?

HECTOR *waits for* NENE *to respond.*

MARIELA: What are you waiting for? Tell her the punchline.

HECTOR: No te awheates!

ANA: (*Laughs.*) Ese sí estuvo bueno, Hector, pero . . .

They wait. NENE *doesn't move.*

MARIELA: Nada. How about you, Ana. She likes it when you make her the center of attention.

ANA: (*With big gestures.*) Aquí está, Adilene! Su candidata para el alcalde de Los Angeles!

They wait. NENE *doesn't move.*

HECTOR: Y si le doy un beso?

ROSIE: Cómo crees, Hector. You really think we're going to let you kiss her.

MARIELA: What about her príncipe? Maybe he can come and kiss Nene.

ANA: Por favor. Nadie la va a besar sin su permiso. Ni príncipe. Ni Hector. Ni Nadie.

HECTOR: What if we play her favorite music?

MARIELA: I think she really likes banda.

ROSIE: Bueno, pues, play it!

Music plays. They wait. No movement in NENE.

ANA: Y si bailamos?
HECTOR: But I don't even know how to dance to this music.

They dance. MAGDALENA *does not dance. She continues her slow motion walk toward* NENE. *No movement in* NENE. *Music stops. They stop dancing.*

MARIELA: Nothing's working. (*Screams.*) Nene!!

MAGDALENA *has reached* NENE *and is standing next to her.*

ROSIE: What are you going to do, Magdalena?
ANA: Déjala. A ver si ella puede hacer algo por Nene.
MAGDALENA: (*Speaking in slow motion.*) Nene. Sabes que me tardo siete minutos en caminar de la puerta de la tienda a mi estación en la caja #1. Tomo exactamente siete pasos. Me tardo un minuto en cada paso. Soy lenta. Yo lo sé. Camino despacio. Trabajo despacio. Yo lo sé. Todos lo saben. Ustedes, los clientes. Pero nadie sabe el por qué. Voy a la clínica y no me lo pueden explicar. Voy al hospital y los doctores solo se quedan con las bocas abiertas. Que es un gran misterio médico. Pero yo tengo una teoría. Creo que los hombres en mi vida me han robado mi velocidad. He conocido las miradas, las mierdas, las manos, los momentos que nos pueden dejar paralizadas. Sé que hay momentos cuando no se puede distinguir entre caricias y golpes. Cada golpe, cada caricia me ha hecho más lenta, Nene. Me quitan de mí un pedazo de mi velocidad. Pero nunca me han dejado así parada. Eso no. Jamás. Y mi hija, no me lo vas a creer, pero ella nació con una supervelocidad. Puede caminar de la casa a la escuela en 2 minutos y son 10 cuadras. Imagínate. Ahora dedico mi vida a cuidar su supervelocidad. Quedar paraliza-

da no es opción, Nene. Qué, no te han dicho, que la gente parada no sirve para nada? Qué te pasó, Nene? Te dijo algo feo, ese señor feo. Van a haber más como él. Y van a haber otros que considerarás amigos, novios, amantes que intentarán dejarte paralizada con una mirada, una mentira, una caricia, un golpe, un insulto, una declaración de amor. Lo importante es seguir adelante. Yo sigo adelante. Despacio. Pero siempre pa' delante. Tú también tienes planes, Nene. Tú también tienes que seguir.

MAGDALENA *begins to exit in slow motion. When she has taken one step,* ANA *exits. When she has taken two steps,* ROSIE *exits. When she has taken three steps,* HECTOR *exits. When she has taken four steps,* MARIELA *exits.* MAGDALENA *exits.*

ROSIE: (*Over loudspeaker.*) Nene . . . Póngase a trapear.

NENE *unfreezes and picks up mop. Music plays.* NENE *starts dancing.*

Publix me hizo reír la primera vez que vi
el letrero. Estudiar los nombres de los super-
mercados es una de las cosas que me gusta

hacer. Sobre todo si son tiendas de las que
nunca he oído hablar. Es que tenemos esos
nombres tan arraigados en nuestros seres

que hasta parece una tontería cuando oyes
a alguien decir otro nombre en ese contexto
familiar. Si uno dice "voy al *Shaw* pa'

comprar un poco de leche" a alguien que
está acostumbrado a decir "voy a *Harris
Teeter* pa' comprar un poco de leche" bien

podría estar diciendo: "Voy a ir al spank" o
"al boink". ¿Cuáles son los nombres de sus super-
mercado favoritos? ¿Qué tal el *Hinky Dinky*?

En algún lugar del sur de Chicago se encuentra
una tienda de abarrotes llamada *Moo y Oink*.

Anónimo
"Lo Voy Hacer" tiene algunas tareas

para hoy. Las ha escrito
ya abajo . . .
     Ir a la oficina de correo.
     Ir al supermercado con una lista.
     —Hablarle a mamá por Skype o, en su defecto,
        escribir un correo electrónico—
     Acordarme de mi amigo obeso con un SMS.
     Limpiar el apartamento.
     Darle de comer a las aves.
ok, he estado durante 2 horas haciendo nada.
Es hora de ponerse a trabajar.

Actualización:
alimentar a los colibríes, ¡el alimentador está vacío!

American Copia

Looks like I'm going to the grocery store for some grapefruit juice tonight to commence with the experiment.

Alma and I dated for a short while. She said that I wasn't allowed to kiss her on or around the UC Berkeley campus because she didn't want our friends and colleagues to find out. Trying to persuade her, I quoted my translation of an old Berkeley postcard, "besarte no es crimen en Berkeley." But she shrugged her shoulders in that immensely adorable way she does when she means "no" but doesn't want to say "no." So I suggested we walk down Telegraph to the parking lot of *Andronico's* on Parker, which would be far enough that no one would be able to see us and know the total of our besos. She said it was too far. "Pero Almis de mi Almis, wouldn't it be worth it?"

In 1966, we go to the supermarket to boycott the Schenley Liquor Company, which owns the vast majority of the vineyards in the San Joaquin Valley. We refuse to buy all table grapes nationwide, and in 1970 the boycott pays off as Schenley Liquor and other grape producers are pressured to sign contracts providing significant benefits to workers. The grape boycott proves that just as Jesus turned water into wine the workers united turned grapes into justice.

I'm going to the grocery store, visit mom, get some keys made, straighten the house, clean the bathrooms and make a nice dinner. That should keep me busy, but if I run out of stuff to do I'll clean out the fridge. It's getting kinda sticky in there.

After the 3rd Annual XWG Noche de Florycanto, Huerta walks with Alurista down Telegraph Avenue in search of a bottle of wine. They buy a bottle at a small market on Telegraph and Dwight and walk back to alurista's hotel room. What was spoken between the two poets will become a matter of great conjecture for Huerta's biographers. When asked about this conversation in an interview, Huerta simply responds, "Hablamos de la poesía, las mujeres y de otros placeres." One of Huerta's biographers will make this encounter a central moment in the chapter "Huerta and the Chicano Tradition."

In the mean time, I'm going to the grocery store to find something I can buy for $1.62—all in pennies, of course. Hopefully you won't be the lucky person that gets stuck behind me at the checkout counter. Should Congress abolish the penny? Please let me know your thoughts!

After a movie, Someone offers to drive me home because she's going that way anyway since she has to stop at the *Safeway* on Rose and Shattuck to buy ingredients for what she calls her "famous Spinach salad." I accept the ride and reply, "You mean your 'famous all over town spinach salad'?" Then Someone says, "Why? Because people question its authenticity?" Someone and I have a good laugh over this—not a carcajada, more like a chuckle. I am of the opinion that a joke explained is a joke misunderstood. So I will simply recommend that you read Marcial Gonzalez's *Chicano Novels and the Politics of Form: Race, Class, and Reification.*

I'm going to the grocery store on my bike, and loading up. Seriously. I'm going to do it.

Marisol has a story about grocery carts: Once upon a time, I was a young, high-achieving, broke, perfectionist, knocked up, unwed, chicana ivy league student (so many stereotypes, so many oxymorons). We had no money, no car, and lied about my baby-daddy (we weren't married yet) being an international (read: wealthy) "mexican" student in order to secure an apartment off campus after i had been denied because i was clearly "not a trust-fund baby." We lived across the street from "la casa," yale's latino cultural center, where i had worked since i started school. Our apt fondly became known as "la casa annex." in any case, our corner place at 129 York St Apt 4G was two blocks downhill from the yale-new haven hospital. since it was common practice for undergrads to "borrow" grocery carts (they call them "carriages" on the east coast) (and post office carts—those big huge ones for the mail! they were super fun to be pushed around in!) to move (a practice in which we participated plenty of times), we decided that if it came down to it, francisco could always just use the grocery cart to push me up the hill to the hospital when i went into labor. After all was said and done, we bought an old station wagon and francisco drove me those two blocks uphill when the time came. But we almost always kept a grocery cart stashed in the bushes from the new *Walgreens* that had just been built across the street. Just in case.

In the 60s Jose Montoya will accompany Gertrude Stein to the supermarket. As they pass the florist shop at the front of the store, Stein will famously proclaim, "A rose is a rose is a rose." Later when he picks up a bag of rice and places it in his basket, Montoya responds, "Arroz is arroz is arroz." This becomes a defining moment for la poesía Chicana. We are to work within the American tradition, but we shall write arroz poéticas on our own terms. On our own terms, ese.

Though to be fair to me, why are people (actually only men) always trying to talk to me when I'm going to the grocery store, walking my dogs, trying to get from the parking lot into my building at work, etc.

I accompany Almis de mi Almis to the *Whole Foods* on Harrison. She starts feeling on peaches to see if they are ripe enough to eat. I grab one of the peaches and pretending to bite it ask her, "Do I dare eat a peach?" She calls me a nerd because she knows it's from T.S. Eliot's "Prufrock" poem. Trying to convince her that I am not a nerd, I sing, "Really love your peaches, wanna shake your tree." But she had never heard of The Steve Miller Band.

Oh and about the grocery. my dad always raised us to keep a "biscuit under your pillow." in the depression, the idea was if you got two biscuits you ate one and the other one you should put under your pillow and save it for the day when you don't have anything to eat. this has become for my dad (and also for me strangely) a reason to save a lot. because one day you never know when you're going to need it.

People's Community Market—For many years, People's Grocery worked toward opening a for-profit grocery store in West Oakland. We incubated and successfully spun off a project to build People's Community Market (PCM) in January of 2010, of which Brahm Ahmadi (co-founder of People's Grocery) is the founder and CEO. We will be one of PCM's partners when it opens its doors in 2012, contributing nutrition programming, leadership development and providing pathways for the store to build relationships with residents.

I actually like going to the grocery store. It's a big, friendly building with meat, cheese and smiling people who say things like "good day" and "may I help you?" It's like a tiny Wisconsin. But I don't like to grocery shop—it's work.

I'm going to the supermarket. What shall I learn of baked beans and baked beans of me?

When he visits Mexico, Pablo Neruda finds the essence of Mexico to be in "los mercados más hermosos del mundo." Sing, Gaby, of the poesy lived in el mercado *Abastos*: Una viejita vende cebollas que trajo de San Juan. Una señora vende pollo de una granja en Zamora donde las gallinas andan libres pero luego les retuercen los pescuezos. Anda el forastero, poeta y vaquero, cantando canciones de traición y desamor. Están los turistas fuereños y adinerados gastando sus dólares en artesanías y chucherías dizque según hechas a mano. Y ahí se pone el chiquillo a vender papitas y chicharrones para los señores que se están tomando sus caguamas y quieren botanear. Y los cuerpos sangrientos de las vacas y los puercos invadiendo la carnicería con el olor de muerto. Y los perros callejeros que mueven las colitas por una borona de tortilla, o por lo menos un pedazo de pan. Otra señora vende elote en vaso. Y pasan los novios agarrados de la mano porque los domingos son los únicos días que los papás dejan salir a la novia. Una niña vende chicles; a los 7 años, todo los días viene aquí a trabajar. Y una estudiante medio pocha escribe versos de lo que observa . . . Me paro en medio del mercado junto al puesto del curandero charlatán que apesta a mirra, a hierba santa maría, a salvia y a copal. Y una mujer indígena me mira y me pregunta, "¿Qué va a llevar, marchantita?" Y me acuerdo que vine a comprar aguacates para comérmelos con tortillita, limón y sal.

West Oakland Grocery Store Project—There is a strong potential that a national warehouse food store chain owned by *Kroger* will be built in West Oakland. People's Grocery has launched an education and organizing campaign to encourage informed public debate regarding the pros and cons of existing and potential retail grocery options for West Oakland. This includes community surveys, public forums, neighborhood dinners and coalition work with concerned organizations and residents.

"Time me!" says little Sara as she runs into the grocery store. Her mom waits for her in the car. While we wait for Sara to return with the items on her list, let us discuss the Global Polio Eradication Initiative and the dreams of a post-eradication world. The GPE Initiative works to ensure that every last child is protected from polio. But its work will not end once polio has been eradicated. Activities will be needed to minimize the risks of poliovirus re-introduction and the emergence of circulating vaccine-derived poliovirus.To prepare for the management of these risks, the GPE Initiative has a multi-pronged programme of work consisting of research, new product development, strategy formulation and policy development. But let us return to the United States, to where Polio has been eradicated, to where Sara is running as fast as her little feet take her back to her mother sitting in the car. Sara plays this game with her mother, who can't run into the store herself because she suffers from polio. It is Sara's job to buy whatever items are needed from the store. Her mother times her. And Sara always tries to beat her best time.

"Go with"—This seems to be a (U.S.) Midwestern (or, at least, Chicago) thing: "I'm going to the grocery store. Do you want to go with?" Arggh! My response often is, "Go with you? Go with money? Go with somebody better looking? Go with a bottle of scotch?"

Baked Apples and Besos—that's what Alma and I titled our third date. My plan was to cook a vegetarian dinner for her, from a recipe for Pasta e Fagioli that I found in *Vegeterian Cooking for Dummies*. I had to go to *Safeway* and *Andronico*'s on Shattuck not only to buy ingredients but also a large pot and dishes because I was in transition and didn't have a fully equipped kitchen. Alma would later compliment my "pasta with beans" as "edible." From another recipe in the same book, I made baked apples and served them with ice cream. I credit this dessert for my first Almis beso. Me dejó tocar su linda cara y besar sus lindos labios. Hence the name of the date, *Baked Apples and Besos*. She and I (she says it was just me) started giving alliterative titles to our dates. First date: *Hiking and Halfprice*. Second date: *Francisco and Fireworks*. I suggested that our fourth date should be *Pineapples and Panties*. She didn't go for it but admitted that would be a fun trip to the supermarket.

Share First Oakland—Our Vision for the Future. We actively promote the creation of home and community gardens, Community Supported Agriculture cooperatives, and neighborhood wholesale buying clubs. We provide funds and training for these and any local, cooperative projects that model the path toward a reliable, sustainable food supply for our inner cities. Please join us. Help feed the hungry!

I'm hungry and thirsty. I'm going to the grocery store. Tell me what to get.

I think there is something strange about people in affluent societies choosing to deny themselves food. It's one thing if you can't afford it. Anthony Braxton chooses to eat unhealthy food because it is cheaper and he can't afford expensive restaurants and health food when he is touring. Going hungry is no joke or stunt or art for millions of people. I like your idea about an undocumented poetics. Another idea is a secret or hidden poetics, as I'm reminded of indigenous people who have had to sometimes keep their real beliefs, their real names and even their languages secret in order to survive.

And I try, too, to cluster errands, so if I'm going to the grocery store and my 2-year-old has been wanting to go to the library, we do it all together in one trip.

So from now on I'm going to go to grocery store every Wednesday and gets lots of good fresh food. I'm going to get a pineapple (my favorite fruit) and eat some tonight . . . ooh I'm so excited!

In Spring 2007, Alma slips and falls on her bum as she walks past the cash registers in the *Safeway* on College and Claremont. This could be an example of what Baudelaire in his essay "On the essence of laughter" calls the "inadvertently comic" because her boyfriend and other people in the store laugh at her. But it could also be an example of "le comique absolu." Baudelaire says, "The man who trips would be the last person to laugh at his own fall, unless he happened to be a philosopher, one who had acquired by habit a power of rapid self-division and thus of assisting as a disinterested spectator at the phenomena of his own ego" (trans. Mayne). Possessing the power of self-doubling and despite the fact that her toosh really hurts, philosophical Alma laughs at herself.

Raza Graduation, UCB. May 2012. So you think you all bad now, Joe. Mr. College Grad. I'm just messing with you. Congratulations. I'm always going to remember that day when we all met: you and me and Melissa. Not just because that's the day I first laid eyes on my Meli— remember what I said after she said goodbye and left the bar? "Absolutely adorable!" Alright, alright, maybe the first thing I actually said was, "Who the heck was that?!" But can you blame a Mexican for being so excited. The girl had jokes, man, talking about, what did the cuchillo say to the jello? And she even indulged my "Funch" idea. You get it? Fun Lunch—yeah, not just because of Meli but because that's the first time you and I actually hung out. And remember what you said when I asked how your first week at Berkeley was going? You said, "Man, I can't find any Kool-Aid." And while you were going on about your supermarket search for Kool-Aid I was thinking this Olmec-head-cabezón might just not make it at UCB. But then, man, you became Big Mexican on Campus. Joseph Ríos. Raza Coord. Recruiting all the little brown ones. Now you're walking across the stage with your mom, and you know your dad is walking right next to you, too. All proud of you, Jojo. And, oh yeah, don't stop believing that some day the Kool-Aid pitcher might just burst through our walls.

Alejandro texts Alma: (1/2) Im at the grocery store & theres this little old lady who was eating samples but whatever she ate she didnt like so she spat it out & put it back on the (2/2) tray. the guy had to wipe down and sanitize everything . . . And there was still some half chewed food that didnt make it in the trash. Haha gross!

To a man, "I'm going to the store" is a declarative sentence —nothing else. There's nothing to "I'm going to the store" that means anything other than "I'm going to the store." To a wife it's an invitation.

Finally, we would like to remind people that the Progressive Workers Organizing Committee is sponsoring a march and rally against war and repression on Saturday, January 25. We will assemble in the *Fiesta* Grocery Store/*Dollar* Store parking lot at 75th Street and Lawndale, Houston, at 1:30 pm. We will then march down 75th Street to Mason Park, where the rally will be held. The demonstration has been endorsed by the International Socialist Organization, Socialist Labor Party— Houston, Montgomery County Green Party, Harris County Green Party and Campus Greens of UH. Other endorsements are forthcoming. English and Spanish versions of the flyer for the event are available. Please get in touch if you would like to endorse the January 25 demonstration, receive more information about our work, or inform us about your activities. We look forward to hearing from you soon. In Solidarity and Struggle.

Tonight I'm going to the grocery store for the first time in like 2 months, and I'm going to get a bunch of fruits and veggies—YUM!

Share First Oakland—What We Do. In collaboration with trusted East Bay direct service providers, we put high-quality, nutritious food onto the tables of Oakland's most vulnerable—the homeless, low-income seniors, people in life recovery, at-risk women and children and economically distressed families. Since 2008 we have distributed more than 200 tons of food.

Animals don't have supermarkets with a department that packages their meat for them. It's about survival and instinct. Do you really think the meat you buy comes from prey that was hunted for you?

At 11:56:39 am, I text Alma to say, "I'm walking around in the fiesta on bellaire and hillcroft." I send a second text, "My life is absurd, alma. I know that sounds melodramatic but it is." She texts back, "From ur grocery store poem? I'm standing in my gym clothes in the women's locker room. Feel good after working out." I text, "Damn, alma." She texts, "Thought that might make you smile ☺", and follows it with this text: "And yes it does sound melodramatic, but that's u." I text, "And by the way the text exchange we just had is going to go in the book." She: "What texting?" I: "The texting we just did starting w me telling u I was at fiesta to this one."

A guy saying "I'm going to the store" usually means "I'm out of beer." Everyone knows that.

Rich-heard Road-ree-guess (This is how he pronounces it; this is how he hears it most often.) goes to the supermarket and experiences an epiphany. Rich-heard Road-ree-guess (This is how he pronounces it; this is how he hears it most often.) discovers that Velveeta has created a product that blends American cheese and Mexican jalapeño. In an interview with Billy Moyer, Rich-heard Road-ree-guess (This is how he pronounces it; this is how he hears it most often.) will remember this epiphany and declare Jalapeño Velveeta to be an American Revolution. Another day, Rich-heard Road-ree-guess (This is how he pronounces it; this is how he hears it most often.) goes to the supermarket and is dumbfounded by the "Ethnic Foods" aisle. As a rebuttal, Rich-heard Road-ree-guess (This is how he pronounces it; this is how he hears it most often.) firmly proclaims, "I am not a can of refried beans." This is what matters to me: the story of the educated brown man who will go to the supermarket everyday unable to satisfy the hunger of memory.

A man is a success if he gets up in the morning and gets to bed at night, and in between he buys what he wants to buy at the grocery store.

As part of her winning entry for the Alfred Arteaga Poetry Prize—a competition conducted by XWG to promote poetry among UC Berkeley Chican@ undergraduates—Cecilia Caballero submits a poem titled "Grocery Shopping." Alfred Arteaga (1950-2008 y PRESENTE) was a poet and professor of Ethnic Studies at UC Berkeley. His books include *Chicano Poetics, Cantos, House with the Blue Bed* and *Frozen Accident*. He was awarded the Pen Oakland Josephine Miles Award and the National Endowment for the Arts Fellowship. Alfred offered an unconditional friendship and mentorship to XWG and its members. As a humble gesture to honor him, our organization has unanimously decided to name our annual florycanto poetry prize after him. Te queremos, Alfred.

"A ver, Almita. ¡¿Qué traes ahí?! No te hagas mensa. A ver, abre las manos. ¡¿Cacahuates?! ¿Y esos? No, Almita, en esta famila no tenemos rateros. Ándale. Regrésalos." A handful of peanuts—this is the only thing Almita has ever stolen. She went with her ma to the grocery store on the day the foodstamps arrived. But hunger travels faster than foodstamps, and it had been days since the hunger had arrived. Her ma will buy only food she can buy with WIC: cheese, milk and eggs. Almita hated those blocks of cheese. She craves more than WIC food, so she reaches into the pile of peanuts and pockets two peanuts. Once outside of the store Almita takes out the two peanuts and cracks one of them. But her plan is spoiled because the peanut has spoiled. Her ma notices she has taken the peanuts y la regaña. She tells Almita to take the peanuts back. (I'm sorry, Almis, that when you told me this story at *Lucky*'s my thoughts were elsewhere.)

Un hombre en mi sueño me dijo
"Tom, voy al súper. ¿Quieres algo?"

Y al instante, me llamó la atención.
Entonces el miedo se puso tan intenso

que parecía llegar a un clímax acompañado
por la mezcla rápida de las voces.

Solo quiero aclarar. Es en mis sueños
que estoy comiendo fuera de control. En mis sueños
voy a la tienda a comprar galletas y helados. Mis sueños
pasan por el supermercado (que solía ser mi debilidad
cuando comía en exceso). Tragarme mis sueños.
Compro bolsas de bagels y muffins en mis sueños.
Donde me trago todo en una sola sesión es en mis sueños.

Meet Memo

Meet Memo, a four-year-old grocery cart. He has never ventured beyond the supermarket parking lot, but the older and more experienced carts speak to him of a time when they were able to cross the yellow line. They speak to him of wild adventures rolling down the Ohlone Greenway. The elder with the rickety left back wheel captivates Memo's attention when he speaks of strangers he met in his journeys. The elder is most fond of an old woman named Soledad. "I was loyal to her. And I carried her belongings in my basket."

Julio, the supermarket employee in charge of corralling the carts, often found Memo—his wheels locked and unable to move—at the edge of the parking lot wondering at the beyond.

"You're lucky, Julio, you get to cross this line and go far from this place every day."

Julio responds, "It's not that great out there. There's only crosswalks and heartbreak."

"I just want to be able to go beyond the yellow line once."

"You belong here, Memo. You serve a purpose here."

"No, I just get pushed around all day." Julio sympathizes with Memo as he knows what it feels like to be pushed around. He disengages the locked wheels and allows Memo to cross the yellow line. "Maybe the beyond will be better to you than it has been to me. Maybe you will find someone to curl up in your carriage."

Memo rolls his way down the Ohlone Greenway. He encounters some middle school kids, who begin to jump up and down on him. One boy jumps inside Memo's carriage and tells his friends to push him. They push fast and faster and ram Memo into a fence. Memo braces for the impact, but he can't stop himself from turning over. He also can't help tossing the small boy into the air. The boy crashes down and hurts his leg. He begins to cry. Some of the kids run away scared. Others help. An adult shows up and carries the boy away.

Memo lies there for a long time until an older woman walks by with two bags full of aluminum cans. She turns him upright and loads the bags. She takes him to another shopping plaza parking lot and dumps the aluminum cans in the recycling machine and gets her money. She leaves Memo behind.

Once he feels safe Memo begins to roll and seek new adventures. He recognizes Julio walking down the street and calls out to him. Julio is talking on his cell and is oblivious to everything else. Memo notices Julio's hand gestures growing more desperate. Julio is at the crosswalk and does not notice the large bus coming at him. Memo sees Julio is in danger and tries to warn him. But Julio seems to be trapped in his own world full of heartbreak. Memo rolls into the street and pushes Julio out of the way. The bus knocks Memo up in the air, and Memo flips and crashes down in the middle of the street. Cars come to a screeching halt.

Julio runs to him and manages to get him onto the sidewalk. Memo takes a while to recover. He has a dent in the front of his basket and his front wheel is bent and crooked. Julio, who is now happy that he and Memo are not too badly injured, escorts Memo back to the supermarket parking lot. Memo is glad to be back home with his family and friends, and he is proud of his dent and his crooked wheel. He talks to the younger carts about his adventures and shows them his battle scars. Memo warns them but entices them, and he can tell that they dream about traveling beyond the yellow line.

Sum of Our Love

My family stops at the 99¢ store on Chimney Rock to get snacks and supplies for our trip to Galveston. Mi Tío Güero and his wife and children have come up from Nuevo Laredo to visit my mother. I place my young cousin Irám, who has been diagnosed with autism and West Syndrome, in the baby seat of the grocery cart and push him up and down the aisles to entertain him.

Irám, you are the youngest child of the youngest child.
Tomás Gómez Magaña marries Domitila Carranza Yera, and they have 12 children.

1. Delia marries Rafael Becerra and they have five children: María del Carmen, Marta Patricia, Rafael, Juana María and Juan Alberto. Delia adopts Arely. Mela marries Omero, and they have one child, Omero Ali. Mela is widowed and marries Willie Valdo, who already has a boy, Willie Valdo. They have one daughter, Sarai. Marta marries Manuel, and they have two children: Kendra and Christopher. Rafa marries Aurora and they have two children: Desire and Jonathan. Juani marries Paco, and they have one child, Paquito. Beto marries Teresa, and they have three children: Claudia Maleini, America and Beto.

2. Pancho marries Hermilinda Alvarado, and they have four children: Francisco Javier, Mayra Xoxitl, Berenice and

Abraham. Francisco Javier marries Ana, and they have two children: Edgar y Jennifer. Xoxitl marries Jose, and they have two children: Daniel and Cecilia. Berenice marries Victor, and they have three children: Victor, Abril and Vicki. Abraham marries Guadalupe, and they have one child, Maximiliano, and are expecting a baby girl.

3. Faustino marries Francisca and they have five children: Noelia and Jazmín—Francisca's daughters from a previous relationship—and César Eliud, Iván de Jesús, and Kenya. Noelia marries René, and they have two children: Alondra y Gamaliet. Jazmín has three children: David Damián, Mónica and Jared. Mónica lives with Eric Pantoja, and they have one child, Eric. César marries Erica, and they have two daughters: Ashley and Leisha Amairani.

4. Emeterio dies in a car accident as an adolescent.

5. Margarita marries Javier, and they have two children: Javier Omar and Tomás Israel. With Salvador Hernández, Margarita has one child, Saul Inocente.

6. Leopoldo marries Nancy, who already has a daughter, Nancy, and they have one child, Iván Alejandro.

7. Juan José marries Maricela Cruz, and they have four children: Juan José, Edgar Fabián, Jorge Alberto and Christian Tomás. Juan José has two other children: Óscar and Héctor. Juan José (mono) has a child, Kelly Joana, before he marries Marlen, and they have two children: Dayan and Christian. Fabián (toña) lives with Alma, who already has one daughter, Yelitza, and they have one child, Kenai. Jorge Alberto (gabacho) marries San Juana, and they have two children: Kiara and Aaron. Christian marries Mayra, and they have two children: Yamilet and Axel Jared.

8. María Ignacia marries Juan Enrique, and they have two children: Luis Enrique and Edna Viridiana. Luis Enrique marries Kerena Juárez, and they have three children: Sheila, Luis Enrique and Santiago. Viri has two children with Fernando: Edna Jacqueline and Fernando. Viri marries Juan Carlos, who already has a son, Carlos.

9. Óscar marries Marta Aredondo, and they have three children: Julián, Mariela and Aleirám. Julián lives with Leslie Canela and they have one child, Daniela Layan.

10. La bebé passes away when she is only 6 days old.

11. Héctor marries Eva, who already has a son, Diego, and they have two children: Adilene and Ivette. Diego marries Zuelem.

12. Sergio marries Rocío Sánchez, and they have three children: Irma Stepany, Eunice and Sergio Irám.

Irám, you
are the sum of our
love. He
laughs. I
look to see
what
has grabbed
his attention and see
a big
sign on the wall, "99
cent store now
open 9
days a week."

"Juan Carlos: fui
al H-E-B con mi mamá
ahorita
regresamos. alístate
pa irnos
al mall ahorita que llegue. Bye:
ate: viri.
Pídele
el tel a mary pa que
me hables.
Tus llaves están ya sabes donde. Ok."

"Don Tomi,
     ¿qué le pasó
          a su tiendita?"

"Todos mis nietos
     se comían
          la mercancía."

Mi amá va a la tienda porque necesitamos
anahorias y **A**
     rroz y **B**
        olillos y **C**
           ilantro y **CH**
              uletas y **D**
                    onas y **E**
                lote y **F**
           rijoles y **G**
      alletas y **H**
   uevos y **I**
     ce cream y **J**
        alapeños y **K**
           iwi y **L**
                eche y **M**
              acaroni y **N**
           ueces y **Ñ**
        ame y **O**
      kra y **P**
    látanos y **Q**
  ueso y **R**
    es y **S**
      odas y **T**
        omates y **U**
           vas y **V**
              ainilla y **W**
                  affles y **X**
              ocolatl y **Y**
         ogurt y **Z**.

I.

"¡¿Por qué no me quieres?!"
Soltó sus gritotes el Fer ahí en el supermercado.
No daba ni pa tras ni pa delante.
Ni sabía que hacer. Tenía los pelos en punta.
"¡¿Por qué no me quieres?!"
José Luis fue el que le dijo,
        "No voy a aguantar tus chiflaciones."
Viri dice que en la casa Fer hizo lo mismo.
Soltó sus gritotes.
"¡¿Por qué no me quieres?!"

II.

"Tía, ¿me compras algo?"
        "¿Y por qué te voy a comprar algo, Fer,
        si no te quiero?"

Una vez a mi tía Rocío
la atropellarron en Reynosa
cuando fue al súper y unos señores
la subieron a la pesera y mi tía iba
con mi prima irma y cuando llegó
a su casa su esposo le preguntó
      ¿qué te pasó?
y ella dijo
      me atropellaron.

American Copia

I'm going to the grocery store right now for fettucini! By the way, I meant to tell you last time I love the music!

"The grocery store," says La Pouty, "is the loneliest place in the world."

Lili is going to the grocery store with pie and Desiderius Erasmus' *Copia* on her mind: I like pie. I'm fond of pastry. I enjoy baked goods. I take pleasure in ingesting sweet comestibles that are like cake but which are not actually cake. That which is baked and fruit-filled brings me joy.

When you were little did you ever play "I'm Going to the Grocery Store"? It was a memorization game where you had to remember alphabetically the contents of a shopping list from A to Z. Children can have fun with the grocery game where they list things starting with the letter A and go through the alphabet. Begin the game by saying, "I'm going to the grocery store and I need apples." The next player must add to the list using the letter B, such as, "I'm going to the grocery store and I need apples and broccoli." Continue going back and forth between players, remembering the list and adding new items until you reach the letter Z.

When La Pouty goes to the supermarket with no one but me, she goes with everyone. When La Pouty goes to the supermarket with everyone but me, she goes with no one.

It's not like I'm going to the grocery store going "hey, everyone look at my fabulous bag." There's more important topics in the world besides who has what.

When she was young, my roommate Tia used to play a game with her Mom called "Hello, friend." Six-year-old Tia would go to the store and pretend to meet her mom.
Mom: "Hello, Friend."
Tia: "Hello, Friend."
Mom: "What are you doing?"
Tia: "I'm shopping."
Mom: "Will you like to share a cart?"
Tia: "Yes. I want to be stranded in a dessert aisle."
Her mom would let Tia shop with her own grocery list. Fondly remembering this game, Tia says that the grocery store loses its magic when one grows up. It's just something that we have to do.

bueno la historia no es muy interesante pero al menos pasó algo / yo no tenía nada de ganas de salir hoy; era uno de esos días en los que estás todo triste y no quieres ver a nadie / pero no tenía comida. // bueno entonces estaba yo escogiendo bagels / y un viejito llega y me dice que la comida chatarra me iba a matar mi belleza jaja / entonces yo sonreí y seguí escogiendo panes / y me pregunta el hombre que si había probado los de sabor pizza porque tendría que comer cosas mágicas para estar tan bonita y tener el pelo así jaja / le dije que no // le di las tenazas y ya / pero el viejito súper tierno como que me devolvió todo el ánimo porque me lo dijo sin ningún interés / supongo me notó triste / claro le di el buen día y una sonrisa.

La Pouty offers to take me to *Trader Joe's* to buy some groceries. She grabs a grocery cart. I grab a grocery cart. She goes down one aisle. I go down a different aisle. I then encounter her by the frozen foods. She doesn't notice me.

I imagine ramming my grocery cart into hers and imagine her pouty eyes looking at me startled as I declare, "Pouty, eres el accidente más bello de mi vida."

The grocery store does not exist. I know. I've been there. La Pouty offers to take me to *Target* in Albany, California, to buy bedding for my new living situation. I buy a set of sheets, pillowcases, comforter and some pillows. She buys some beer on special. I'm not sure now what type of beer she bought, but it is the same beer that she would pack for us along with sandwiches from a Laotian deli by her house that day more than a month later, that day at the Berkeley Marina when we grew old together if only for a second, that day that I would come to know as el día más chistoso de mi chistosísima vida. Ja! Ja! Ja! waves crashing against the rocks; the Golden Gate Bridge and the City of San Francisco out in the distance; mi declaración de amor; tu declaración de amor Ja! Ja! Ja! you saying you feel like you won the lottery; me thinking I hope she knows I have absolutely no wealth; you saying you feel like a little girl; me thinking is that a good thing or a bad thing Ja! Ja! Ja! keeping ourselves warm in your rebozo; abrazándote; más besototes; nuestra risa Ja! Ja!Ja! la lluvia sprinkling from the heavens; los colores del arco iris Ja! Ja! Ja! Ja! Ja! But in the *Target* parking lot while I placed my new bedding in the trunk of your car and you placed the beer in your backseat, that laughter had not yet reached us, my Pouty and me.

John: I grew up in the suburbs so big grocery stores were the norm for me. In college, I had a friend from New York, and one time we went to a *Wegman's* in West Windsor, NJ, and she said, "Oh, I love the grocery stores in the country—they're so huge!" I've always loved them too because they're monuments to abundance. I think the safest I might ever feel is in the produce aisle of a suburban grocery store.

Rachel, my roommate of two weeks when I was subletting a room in a two-bedroom apartment on Bonita Street, goes to the *Safeway* on Rose and Shattuck early in the morning to get some boxes for her move. She tries taking some of the boxes back in a cart but the cart locks its wheels once she passes the yellow line. She tries a second cart before she realizes that the cart is a smart cart that has been engineered to prevent the theft of grocery carts. She will study it with the interest of a scientist —she studies Nueroscience at UC Berkeley—and will declare the smart grocery cart to be the most intriguing innovation in mechanical engineering in recent times.

I enjoy a mix of comfort and style, and even if I'm going to the grocery store in my sweats, I'll still have a feminine piece of jewelry or hair accessory on.

Several days after she takes back her declaration of love by saying her heart was "healing and confused," La Pouty meets with Huerta for a study session at a tea place on San Pablo. She reads a big academic book; Huerta grades papers. When they are done, Huerta offers to walk her home. They pass by *Mi Tierra Foods* where a Xican@ mural has just been completed. La Pouty mentions how she intended to take photos of the mural at various stages of completion to document the process. It is at this point that Huerta realizes the reason why he is madly in love with La Pouty: because going with her to the supermarket to buy groceries together is beyond his imagination. Misunderstanding this statement, Huerta's biographers will make no mention of La Pouty.

Porque eres mi broder de otra moder, I will respect your wishes not to be included. Pero, broder, don't you think it's important to write about how you ran into some woman at a Nicaraguan supermercado 10 years after you dated her, how she was 18 years young when you dated her and she had just broken up with her older abusive married boyfriend, how she worked at the supermarket giving out samples, how when you saw her 10 years later she was holding a baby and she told you that she had married that same abusive guy she used to cry about, how after talking to her you looked at your hands and realized for the first time that they had aged 10 years. Y broder, should I not write about that time when I didn't have any money on me after the gym after we had ran for an hour on the treadmill and you offered to buy me a smoothie, but because all the smoothie places in the East Bay were closed we ended up going to *Lucky*'s and you bought me a 32oz power drink. Should I keep silent about how when you met a young Mexican female supermarket employee, she mistook your question about laundry detergent as an invitation to dance naked, and how when she pointed at the powder she meant to say, *I want you to touch me this same night*. Es que, broder, estas son cosas que se tienen que contar. And should we not record this for our own histories, how in 1988 you crossed the shallow river into Brownsville, USA, how you and 35 other mojados walked across the rocks of the river under full view of a military base—"esos no son nada," the coyotes reassured you—how you climbed out of the third world and onto a *Ralph's* Supermarket parking lot, how you and the other 35 mojados rushed to the vans that were to take you to a cheap motel, how the Americans loading their groceries into their cars stared at you, how you didn't have the time to notice whether those stares rejected or welcomed you.

Tonight La Pouty will go to the supermarket to buy coffee and not once will she think of me.

Late at night, once, Ruth and her husband went to the *Stop 'N Shop* in Amherst, Mass. There was only one manned check-out line, and it was full, so they went through the self check-out line. There's a computerized female voice that says the item that you're buying as you scan it, and instructs you to place whatever it is on the conveyer belt. The machine was on the fritz, and it kept calling out the wrong item. Ruth and her husband got quite a kick out of this, especially when the voice said, "Please Place Your—Nuts—On The Belt" after they'd scanned a loaf of bread.

Help! I'm going to the grocery store. I'm trying to lose weight, so I want to know what you guys snack on that is healthy.

The day I heard La Pouty was happy with another man I went to the supermarket and stuck a can of shaving cream under my shirt and walked out of the store without paying for it.

In a prison interview broadcast today on ABC's *20/20*, Mullins announced that God has forgiven him for the murder, while his victim will spend eternity in Hell for being a homosexual. "It just seemed like the thing to do," said Mullins of his decision to lure Gaither from a bar, cut his throat with a pocketknife, beat him to death with an axe handle, then set his corpse aflame in a ditch. "It didn't seem any different than waking up and saying, I'm going to the grocery store this afternoon. I didn't think he needed to live any longer."

Helpful Words to Know and Use. Brought to you by the Berkeley Student Food Collective. Sustainable: practices which can be carried out indefinitely without causing irreversible damage or resource depletion. Ecologically

Sound: behaviors that are in line with natural processes and inflict minimal or no harm on the environment. Food System: a web of individuals, organizations and other institutions that produce, process and distribute food; the journey from seed to plate and back. Collective: owned and run by a group of people with a common goal. Healthy: taking conscious actions to strike a balance between mental, emotional and biological well-being.

For the Holiday season, I mail La Pouty a greeting card with a $50 *Trader Joe's* gift card. Es que soy terco, Pouty, y sigo pensando que tu corazón es de miguelito. I decide on a supermarket gift card because at least she will get something practical out of my impractical love. Why impractical? She has requested that I not tell her anymore that I am madly in love with her. She may, I believe, even have a new boyfriend. I respect her wishes and make no mention of love anywhere on the greeting card, simply wish health and happiness for her and her loved ones. As for the gift card, I fill it in like this.

To: La Pouty
From: Ja!Ja!Ja!vier
Amount: más que los demás
I'm not writing about love. I'm writing about the grocery store. I hear *Trader Joe's* has frozen mangoes for your smoothies.

Whether I'm going to the grocery store or reading books to children at a book festival, life has taught me not to underestimate the power of thinking ahead.

You know what's funny, last night I had a dream about going to the super market. I was with my mom, trying to get her to buy me stuff to bring back home. Having her spend so I could save. And she took me to a latino grocery store (because she said things were cheaper), and a lot of the produce was wilted. Or they were trying to pass some stuff off as being something it wasn't. For instance I wanted radishes, but the radishes there were actually turnips. And the things that were a bargain price were poor quality, like the old produce, and the stuff that I wanted (like 100% watermelon juice) was incredibly over-priced.

Moral of the story is that if I'm going to the grocery store, I take the Prius, but if I'm going out to the lake, I take the sports car. End of story.

A supermarket gift card makes sense to me because it does not have to be too big of an intrusion in La Pouty's life. She can either choose to purchase groceries or she can roll her pouty eyes and throw the gift card in the trash. Everyday I walk the aisles at *Trader Joe's* hoping she has chosen to use the gift card, hoping for a glimpse of her pouty smile. One day I notice that I have just missed her. Bananas have spoiled, cucumbers softened, ice cream melted, lettuce wilted, milk cartons drooped, the bell broken and the cashier working the express lane has crossed her arms and refuses to lift her head. O Pouty, why must everything you touch turn to poutiness.

He came to live with his brother. He has a very big dog. He knows how to ride a bike. He wanted to find a job. He wanted to talk to his boss. He went to the post office. His wife is at work right now. His wife worked in the house. I am too busy to talk today. I bought a blue car today. I came to _____ (city) today for my interview. I count the cars as they pass by the office. I drive a blue car to work. I go to work everyday. I have three children. I know how to speak English. I live in the State of _____. I want to be a U.S. citizen. It is a good job to start with. My car does not work. She can speak

English very well. She cooks for her friends. She is my daughter, and he is my son. She needs to buy some new clothes. She wanted to live near her brother. She was happy with her house. The boy threw a ball. The children bought a newspaper. The children play at school. The children wanted a television. The man wanted to get a job. The teacher was proud of her class. The white house has a big tree. They are a very happy family. They are very happy with their car. They buy many things at the store. They came to live in the United States. They go to the grocery store. They have horses on their farm. They live together in a big house. They work well together. Today I am going to the store. Today is a sunny day. Warm clothing was on sale in the store. We are very smart to learn this. We have a very clean house. You cook very well. You drink too much coffee. You work very hard.

La Pouty sends me a text to tell me she is "At andronicos" buying "Garlic. Soy creamer. Bow tie pasta. Tomato soup 4 dinner. Not doritos." I text back: "Eit, Pouty, cuídate cuando me mandes un text desde el supermercado porque tal vez un día tus antojos ("I was dead serious about the Doritos," she says.) serán analizados por académicos." Y esta hambre de La Pouty durará por siglos.

You know those guys that hang out in the parking lots of grocery stores and on street corners with clipboards and ask you for money to support their basketball team/community group/whatever? One time Ben was at *Safeway* and passed a couple of those dudes in the parking lot. Then when he was buying some beers he saw another one of them, clipboard in hand, just staring at the premium liquor that they have locked up behind the safety glass. He was swaying a little and his eyes were all weird. He looked back at Ben and then punched the safety glass with his bare fist. When it didn't break he stumbled back a few steps and looked kind of confused, then took a run at it and tried again. You could feel the whole shelf shake, you could tell this guy was hitting it really hard. Then he did it again. It made a lot of noise, but it was Saturday night and the store was pretty empty, so no one noticed, or they pretended not to. The creepy thing was that he kept on looking at Ben the whole time. Ben eventually went around and told the cashier about it, who called someone on his intercom thing. Ben went back to check, but the guy was gone. It was scary but you've got to kind of admire the kind of guy who walks right past a hundred unsecured bottles of liquor to try to punch his way through an inch of safety glass with his bare hands to get at the good stuff.

[Porque me lo has pedido, Pouty, aquí dejo este simple space para que expreses tus ideas del supermercado]

You can buy La Pouty's love at the supermarket. It is both on sale at a discount price, and it is priceless.

Honey, I'm going to the grocery store and I'll be back in 45 minutes, if the Lord wills.

Zoinks! My drummer buddy just called—it's his 39th B-day today! I'm going to the grocery store to get some coffee for tomorrow morning (and maybe ask Impossibly Hot Girl out) and go meet my buddy and his wife for a drink. I haven't had a lot of sleep this week, so it's probably going to be a very short Friday night for me.

La Pouty insists that she is a real person and not just one of my supermarket metaphors. Te equivocas, Pouty. You do not exist beyond the aisles of my grocery store.

Así
que me fui
un poco
loco
en este caso. Me sentía muy triste después de oír
del asesinato de Benazir
Bhutto. No puedo creer la suerte que tenemos de vivir
en sociedades democráticas, incluso
con sus defectos.
No puedo imaginar vivir en un lugar
donde tenía que cuestionar
mi seguridad y la existencia o si no iba
a haber un atentado suicida
en el mercado ese día. No
tengo pan. Y voy
a ir a la tienda hoy
y ni una vez cuestionaré mi seguridad en el camino.

Dos 11s de septiembre han pasado, y todavía
me paseo por mi barrio todos los días
de la misma manera. Si voy a la tienda
de comestibles, entonces a la salida
de mi edificio doy vuelta a la derecha
y camino por la calle Shrader
rumbo a la Haight, paso Amoeba Música
a la izquierda y directamente a Comestibles Cala,
pero si voy a comprar cigarrillos o caminar
a la librería me giro a la izquierda y camino
por la calle Cole rumbo a la Haight. Cuando
me voy por este camino paso por el Bill Graham Centro
de Salud y Recuperación y eso es cuando
lo veo —una pequeña formación
y la disminución
de los arbustos y las flores
muertas en homenaje a los homeless.

el audio caja negra de los pilotos
lo que me llama más
conversar con los controladores de tráfico aéreo
lo que me llama más
el aterrizaje en el Río Hudson
lo que me llama más
el video del vuelo 1549
lo que me llama más
la calma en la voz del capitán Sullenberger
lo que me llama más
el mismo tono con el que yo le diría a mi marido
"voy a la tienda de comestibles"

Realmente
tengo miedo de perder a la gente
que quiero. Así que asegúrese de decir "te amo" antes
de ir al supermercado a comprar pasta de dientes.
He visto programas como televidente
donde muchas personas no lo dicen lo suficiente.
Y entonces alguien muere en un accidente.

La semana pasada,
mientras que revisaba
los elementos
de almacenamiento,
encontró un viejo set
de palos de golf.

"La última vez
que jugué con ellos mis socios
de negocios
estaban vivos", dijo.

"Ahora están muertos,
y yo voy al supermercado.
La vida continúa".

Oráculo

1.

Yo he sido un agente especial de la Oficina Federal de Investigación desde noviembre de 1997. Actualmente estoy asignado a las investigaciones relacionadas con crímenes violentos y otras violaciones de las leyes federales. Hago esta declaración jurada en apoyo de una queja contra Jared Lee Loughner por violaciones de un cargo de intento de asesinato de un Miembro del Congreso, en violación del Título 18, Código de Estados Unidos Sección 351 (c); Cargos 2 y 3, el asesinato de un funcionario y empleado de los Estados Unidos, en violación del Título 18, Código de Estados Unidos, Secciones 1114 y 1111, y cargos 4 y 5 ~ Intento de asesinato de un Funcionario y empleado de los Estados Unidos, en violación del Título 18, Código de Estados Unidos, Secciones 1114 y 1113.

2.

En o alrededor del 08 de enero 2011, en Tucson, Arizona, la congresista Gabrielle Giffords organizó un evento pre-anunciado titulado "El Congreso en Su Esquina", en una tienda *Safeway* en 7170 N. Oracle Road. Congresista Giffords representa el Octavo Distrito en el sur de Arizona. La oficina de la congresista Giffords había publicado el evento por adelantado, incluidos los anuncios de correo y anuncios telefónicos. El miembro del personal de la congresista Giffords declara, "en el evento contó con Gabriel Zimmerman, Ron Barber, Pamela y Simon, que son empleados de los Estados Unidos". Todos asistieron para ayudar a la congresista Giffords en sus funciones oficiales. En enero de 2011, el declarante habló con EE.UU. Mariscal David Gonzales, quien indicó que el Honorable John M. Roll, Juez Jefe de el Tribunal Federal de Distrito para el Distrito de Arizona, ha trabajado con la congresista Giffords en los últimos meses para resolver cuestiones relacionadas con el volumen de casos presentados en el Distrito de Arizona. El Juez Roll fue notificado del caso de la congresista Giffords por teléfono en o alrededor del 07 de enero 2011. Después de haber hablado con Pia Carusone, el Jefe Mayor de Estado de la congresista Giffords en Washington DC, EE.UU. Mariscal González informa que Ron Barber, un miembro del personal de la congresista Giffords, estuvo presente en el evento, dijo que el Juez Roll asistió al evento y trató de hablar con la congresista Giffords, y habló con el Sr. Barber sobre temas relacionados con el volumen de casos federales en el Distrito de Arizona; Juez Roll expresó su agradecimiento al Sr. Barber por la ayuda y el apoyo que la congresista Giffords había dado. Su declarante ha revisado un video de vigilancia digital que narra los eventos en el *Safeway*. En el video el Juez Roll se ve hablando durante varios minutos con el Sr. Barber.

3.

Basado en mi revisión del video y otra investigación, el declarante afirma que aproximadamente a las 10:11 AM el 8 de enero de 2011, Jared Lee Loughner le disparó al miembro del Congreso Gabrielle Giffords, a Gabriel Zimmerman y al Honorable John M. Roll, Juez Jefe del Tribunal de Distrito para el Distrito de Arizona; Simon Pamela, el asistente personal de la congresista Giffords, y Ron Barber, un miembro del personal de la congresista Giffords, así como a aproximadamente 14 personas adicionales. Tanto Pamela Simon Barber y Ron fueron ejecutados y heridos seriamente por Loughner. Después de recibir un disparo de Loughner, Gabriel Zimmerman y Juez Roll murieron por las heridas y la congresista Giffords fue herida de gravedad.

4.

Loughner fue detenido en el lugar y desarmado. En la escena, la policía recuperó el arma utilizada por Loughner, una pistola semiautomática Glock. La Oficina de Alcohol, Tabaco y Armas de Fuego (ATF) ha determinado que Loughner compró la pistola Glock, número de serie 699 PWL, en o alrededor del 30 de noviembre 2010, de la Galería del Deportista en Tucson. Además de la investigación llevada a cabo por la ATF, se corroboró que Loughner compró el Glock por recibos de las tiendas y de video, entre otras pruebas.

5.

El 8 de enero de 2011, una orden de allanamiento fue ejecutada en 7741 N. Avenida Soledad en Tucson, Arizona, donde reside Loughner. Algunas de las evidencias incautadas resultaron en la ubicación de una carta en una caja fuerte, dirigida a "Loughner, Sr. Jared", en 7741 N. Soledad Avenida, de la congresista Giffords, con sello del Congreso, de fecha 30 de agosto de 2007, dándole las gracias por asistir a un evento de "Congreso en la Esquina" en el centro comercial Colinas en Tucson. También se recuperó en la caja fuerte un sobre con la carta en el sobre afirmando "yo he planeado todo con anticipación" y "mi asesinato" y el nombre "Giffords", junto con lo que parece ser la firma de Loughner.

When I Step, Females Respond

When I step females respond. So the other day when I saw this cutie at *Safeway* I knew she was checking me out. She was behind me in line. I knew I'd seen somewhere before. So while I'm paying for my groceries, I can sense she's looking at me —and when I step females respond—so I look back at her. Now we're smiling at each other and I'm paying for my groceries. So right there at the checkout, I ask her, "Do I know you from somewhere?"

She tried to play it off, but I knew she remembered me —because when I step—and sometimes even when I don't —females respond. So I wait for this cutie to pay, you know females like it when you're polite, and I get her name, Monica, and her phone number. She says we should hang out. I told you, when I step, females respond. She says maybe we can take a walk, go to farmer's market. And I'm like that's cool because I just want to see her again.

So we met up at *Au Coquelet*. On University. She was late, but it's cool because I could tell she took long getting ready. I could see that she was really into me—you know, when I step, females respond. We talked. I asked her questions because females like it when you ask them questions and, you know, I'm a nice guy. I told her I was a bouncer, that I was in the navy, and that I was learning how to make jeans to start my own company. And she told me about herself, but then she just like that she had to go. So I ask her, "Why you gotta run?"

I couldn't understand this girl. I texted her because I wanted to let her know that I was into her. And she just kept saying that she was busy. Then one day I'm with my boy on Telegraph and I run into her, and she's with her girlfriends. I still wanna hook up with her, but I don't want to let her think she got to me. So I start expressing myself, you know what I mean, "who does this girl think she is? I'm a pretty good looking guy. Usually when I step, females respond."

So then her girlfriends notice me, and they can see I'm like a pretty good looking guy, I'm nice to look at. They're admiring me and telling this girl to see me again. So the girl agrees to see me again, but I'm not surprised because when I step, females respond.

We were supposed to go to the observatory, but when the day came she didn't want to go. It was like she was afraid of me or something, so I asked her if it was because I was beautiful. She just laughed at me so I start thinking she's just nervous because I'm a pretty good looking guy. So I want to make her feel comfortable. I tell her, "Wow, you're actually attractive." But this girl laughed.

So I ask, "Why you laughing? Why you gotta make it so hard, Monica? Monica, why you being this way?" So we take a walk and talk, and I know that she must be insecure because I look this good.

"Monica, I get it, you're probably feeling insecure. You think I'm going to hit it and split. And that as soon as you give it up, I'm going to walk out the door."

But she didn't say anything.

So I'm wondering what is up because when I step, females respond. Then I thought maybe she doesn't go to bed with dudes, maybe she doesn't get down like that. So I tell her, "Oh, I get it, I get it, you're like a little prude. But you don't have to worry, I look really good naked but I'm also a nice guy. Even all the guys at the gym tell me I look good naked. You haven't even touched on me. How do you know if you haven't touched on me."

Then we're sitting on a rock, and this bitch looks like she rather be somewhere else. I'm getting frustrated now because usually when I step, females respond. So I didn't want to play her games anymore. If she's insecure and shy, that's her problem. When I step, females respond. So I tell her, "That's it. You're not gonna give me nothing. That's really cold. I guess I'm just gonna go." I start to leave and this bitch tells me to have a good day. So I turn around and say, "No, I'm not gonna have a nice day."

Cuando el mono 24 se escapa
del Centro de la Investigación de Tulane
National Primate la semana pasada, los residentes
de Covington conservan el sentido de humor.

"La gente me llama diciendo,
'voy al supermercado, ¿debo
recoger naranjas o plátanos?'"
dice el director del centro Dr. Andrew Lackner.

Por desgracia, Mr. Whipple ha fallecido.
Supongo que antes de profundizar
demasiado hay que tener un momento
para señalar el paso de un icono estadounidense.
Los comerciales de Charmin son algunos
de mis primeros recuerdos. Cuando yo era
un muchacho joven mi hermana trabajaba
en el supermercado local y todas las chicas compra
(así se hacían llamar, en ese entonces)
le llamaban al manager de la tienda "Whipple".
30 años después, estoy de compras en ese
mismo establecimiento (en una nueva ubicación)
y haciendo ojitos a una de las chicas compra.
¡Un brindis a usted, Mr. Whipple! Gracias por las risas
y por sugerir un producto de baño de calidad.
Sí, claro, ella es demasiado joven para mí.

American Copia

Right after I get these damn kids out of my yard I'm going to the grocery store in my dickies and house shoes.

MóTO has been turned loose unto the world, and whilst in it, saw a man's crack @ the *H-E-B*, had the barista @ the drive through nearly fall out of the window trying to talk to me as i drove off & managed to see maribel off to mexico for a few days.

The store's geographical location is quite convenient for most Austinites in the central area. It is located right in the heart of the Guadalupe IBIZ District, a shopping sphere of forty-nine locally owned businesses.

"It's a question of money," Dr. Adam Drewnowski, director of the Center for Public Health Nutrition in the University of Washington School of Public Health and Community Medicine, said. "The reason healthier diets are beyond the reach of many people is that such diets cost more. On a per calorie basis, diets composed of whole grains, fish and fresh vegetables and fruit are far more expensive than refined grains, added sugars and added fats. It's not a question of being sensible or silly when it comes to food choices, it's about being limited to those foods that you can afford."

For instance, a woman might say, "I'm going to the grocery store and I'll be back home soon, probably before five." In the same situation, a man might say, "Going to the store. Back soon." The same idea is conveyed, but men tend to get on with it.

MóTO: important lesson . . . walking alone in the dark to fiesta at midnight is not a good idea . . . no matter how much of a badass i think i am DR: What happened Monica? You live next door. MóTO: yes i do live next door . . . but a man in a red pickup tried to give me a ride home in the empty parking lot . . . btw i'll be free to catch up after ACL this weekend.

These purchases go beyond food however. In the middle of the store is a separate counter of non-consumptive household products. Such as herbal remedies, a selection of ethnic hand-made cloths and the popular product of bamboo utensils. This desire to look and live primitively is contradictory to the actual class and race of people that proudly buy these goods. The products situated at this counter are exclusive to those who purchase these selections frequently, as it is in an obscure area of the store.

Here in Minnesota there is a controversy around the genetic engineering of wild rice. Here we have corporations and scientists wanting to document and codify and then alter or "improve" and ultimately patent or "own" a plant and food source that has been around for thousands of years, providing sustenance to people. What does it mean to be documented? My family emigrated from Germany in the 19th century. My immigrant status has a pedigree, but why does that give me any more rights as a human being than Hsieh? One more note: My wife and I recently watched the movie *The Visitor*. I thought it was an excellent look into what it means to be "undocumented." lov and undrstanding (nvr giv up!) stv ptrmir no man's land minnapolis, mn usa.

MF: for your b-day, we are going to find you a new mattress. MóTO: only if you call the *H-E-B plus*.

What's your philosophy on carrying cash? My philosophy is to only carry around enough cash for what I need during that day. For example, if I know I'm going to the grocery store, I'll bring enough money to get the groceries.

It just so happens there's no food in this place and I'm going to the grocery store tomorrow with or without your lousy permission.

MóTO enjoyed eating her french chaumes while watching where the wild things are, but realized that now she goes to wheatsville too much. they know her name & her sandwich. JD: there's no such thing as too much wheatsville! CS: i miss that MóTO: you miss the wheatsville? or overpriced cheese? austin misses you. hope you come home soon.

Hunger Art: Making gourmet out of something distinctly non-gourmet. Arroz con Bumblebee tuna. Spam sammiches. Spaghetti with ketchup. Maybe I'm limiting myself, or showing my crotchety viejo side, but I am far more interested in the everyday acts of survival from mothers and fathers and kids with no means but the meager work they can find and turn into meager foodstuffs. The fake starvation art stuff, paid or not, is highly ironic when it's done in a country where one can STEAL any variety of bread imaginable. Once you're past that realization . . . and it's not a particularly earth-shattering one . . . the rest is pure artifice. I simply can't understand why one would put him/herself in the position of having to defend suffering as an artistic medium, unless the artists in question donated those honorariums to *actual needy people.*

Do you eat tomatoes? Then listen up————————> *Publix,* a supermarket chain across the Southeast, is a place where shopping is oppression. Coalition of Immokalee Workers (CIW) are asking *Publix* to pay just one cent more per pound for the tomatoes they sell in their stores. *Un centavo más,* seriously. I find pennies on the ground all the time and I'm sure *Publix* management has more than a few lying around. The point is that by paying just one cent more, the tomato farmworkers in Immokalee will receive better wages and working conditions, plus the victorious example of how collective action can hold corporate profit interests accountable. On March 5, 2011, 1,500 workers, community members, students and allies came together to march six miles in protest against *Publix.* I was alongside these folks, and after driving 24 hours straight in the bible belt it was a caffeine pill that kept me lucid but the energy of the crowd that kept everyone going. It was encouraging to have Florida drivers honk their support. Also, the faith groups who have taken on the campaign are a good example of solidarity. However, it was the finale of the teatro popular that was the best part. Especially seeing all the little kids, children of immigrants and allies, be part of a struggle they have yet to fully understand. Overall, it went very well. The CIW and Student Farmworker Alliance did a great job with organizing the event, so yay for them. Anyways, if you shop at *Publix* or know someone who shops at *Publix.* If you eat tomatoes on your nice low-cal salad. If you have any piece of human dignity in you. Then, I encourage you to stop shopping at *Publix.* At least until they get their morality in check, which it seems they feel they are too nice to be fair and, frankly, just don't care about the workers. By doing so, you will be supporting the path for fair food! Do the right thing.

It just so happens there's no food in this place, and I'm going to the grocery store tomorrow with or without your lousy permission.

An excerpt from "Queer in Gringolandia" by Mónica Teresa Ortiz: "Whitesville." This is where I shop, where I eat a popcorn tofu chicken sandwich with cashew tamari dressing, where I buy fair trade organic dark roast coffee, where I purchase a $5 bar of soap that promises to make me smell like a cowboy. The shoppers are mostly white. Gringos we might say. Japanese use the word gaijin to refer to foreigners. All of them, a united group of persons not from Japan, not native to the shores of the island. Considering that I came from the place that used the Boeing B-29 Super Fortress, a four-engine legend that Dresdened the country of Japan, I became a member of the outside persons. This makes perfect sense that I belong to the category of other, of not like you, and not like them. A queer Mexican. That's who I am. Once, while shopping at Whitesville, I ordered a Boar's Head roasted chicken sandwich with provolone, and they asked me my name, and I said, Mónica. Five minutes later, they called out "Juanita!" and I laughed at the absurdity that MON-ih-kuh turned into wa-NEE-tuh. That at Whitesville, where I can buy gluten-free cookies, they can't remember my name or can't pronounce it, that my favorite cashier is a Chicano kid from Corpus Christi with curly hair and a gender neutral queer P.O.C. from Washington State who went to the Evergreen College. Neither speak Spanish, but both feel brown. Because we are both brown in Gringolandia. Even if we went "back to where we came from" we too would be gringos. We would be Americans in Mexico. We would be gaijin.

Accessibility to the store is not a problem, due to public transportation and proximity to campus. In fact there are five bus stops within walking distance from the store, including the 1L/M which is the busiest line with the most stops.

MóTO is so glad that fiesta carries my favorite body wash. now i can smell good!

I have never seen anyone purchase meat as it would be a social stigma to do so in this environment. Interesting enough is that these organic fair trade products come at an inflated cost, therefore is it restricted to a particular class of people who can afford to shop and eat healthy. Many of these fair trade products, as exclusive selections, come from the global south which is prominently poor and black.

Reb Livingston comments on the thread for Wanda Coleman's *Harriet* post, "Of Poetry and Assholes": "Rich, you're absolutely right, there's a long way to go and the answer isn't less voices and outlets. What I don't understand is how any poet would want to move back toward the direction of authority and a 'genuine' kind of thinking toward poetry. I don't understand how a poet would want to move one teeny inch back toward that. And when do uniformed assholes only have voice on the internet? I regularly read reviews and commentary in *The New York Times*, *Poetry* and many other "legitimate" print publications that make me weep. Hell, I can't even get to the grocery store without coming across at least one uninformed asshole. Uninformed assholes are not exclusive to and had pulpits long before the internet."

Grocery store poets do not automatically know the work of other grocery store poets. For further reading: Kim Addonizio, "Quantum," "Onset"; Elizabeth Alexander, "Boston Year"; John Ashberry, "The Skaters," "Others

Shied Away"; Rachel Beck, "Par Avion"; Charles Bernstein, "A Test of Poetry"; Winston Black, "The Grid of Perspective as Applied"; Stephanie Brown, "Allegory of the Supermarket"; Cecilia Caballero, "Grocery Shopping"; The Clash, "Lost in the Supermarket"; Joshua Clover, "Poem: I Come Across the Paving Stones," "Ça Ira"; Eduardo C. Corral, "Ditat Deus"; Ben Doyle, now Ben Doller, "Manna"; Robyn Ewing, "Travelogue #9-S: Glossy Vacation Hero Missing!"; John Espinoza, "Learning Economics at Gemco"; Carolyn Forché, "Return"; Tess Gallagher, "Linoleum"; Allen Ginsberg, "A Supermarket in California"; Renee Gladman, "Proportion Surviving"; Oscar Hahn, "Sociedad de consumo"; Bill Holm, "In the Sauðárkrókur Supermarket"; Randall Jarrell, "Next Day," "A Sad Heart at the Supermarket"; Quraysh Ali Lansana, "Aunt Rubie Goes to Market"; James Laughlin, "Crystal Palace Market"; Amy Lowell, "The Grocery"; Walter McDonald, "The Corner Grocery Store"; Eileen Myles, "Peanut Butter"; Kristin Naca, "Grocery Shopping with my Girlfriend who is not Asian"; Robert Pinsky, "Pig-in-a-Blanket"; Sina Queyras, "Acceptable Dissociations"; Jill Richards, "Five for a Dollar: *Safeway* Sonnets"; Reina María Rodriguez, "first time"; Matthew Rohrer, "Poem About People"; Tomaž Šalamun, "History"; Barbara Schmitz, "Uniforms"; Jefferey Schultz, "J. Finds in His Pockets Neither Change Nor Small Bills"; Bruce Springsteen, "Queen of the Supermarket"; Paula Taylor, "green grocer"; Ann Waldman, "Giant Night"; Dara Wier, "I Write a Book"; Dean Young, "Reentry," "Not in Any Ha-Ha Way"; Kevin Young, "Ode to the Midwest."

MóTO: mexico if you win today i promise to buy a mexican jersey from fiesta & wear it until you lose later AHD: Ditto. MóTO: & then they didnt win! AS: Ja, ja, ja, please buy me one too. MóTO: ja because the colombians didnt even make the world cup. you can be an unofficial mexican too

On her status update, Jennifer Reimer writes, "Going to the grocery store." I comment, "You know I have that copyrighted, right?" She responds saying that she should be able to use that phrase since she analyzed my *Copia* piece in a paper she presented on a panel on "latino" "experimental" "writing"at the Chicago 09 AWP conference. Reimer partly argues, "Huerta builds off his foundational sentence, sometimes faithfully revising the original syntax and sometimes dispensing with the original syntax all together. Yet, each of his sentences probe the relationships between citizenship, consumerism, family, romantic love and personal identity. Personal identity is an equally unstable category for Huerta: the poem's point of view constantly shifts to accommodate his many identities: as undocumented, as naturalized, as graduate student, as son, brother, nephew, as lover, as consumer, as poet. Supermarkets become destabilized chronotopes for exploring the boundaries of nation and identity. Huerta is continually questioning, revising, defining his position in relation to the cultural and national boundaries drawn between piñatas and elote, popsicles and bonbons."

The supermarket's surrounding area also provides designated lanes for bikers and has paved sidewalks.

MóTO: i am going off the grid for awhile. having an adventure in mexico city is of the utmost importance. until i return. & no, christopher, do not pay any ransom if asked. RM: Monica, have fun, explore, be safe, write and eat delicious tacos only Mexico City could offer! MóTO: ah renee you forgot the most important one . . . dont forget to fall in love. thank you though for the well wishes.

RM: All of those will lead you there! :) ciao! CN: Mexico city is hardly off the grid! I expect updates and pics! Have fun guys. JC: Yeah Carla is right, I was surprised at how many places had wi-fi when I was there 2yrs ago. MóTO: i didnt say DF was off da grid, i said i was going off. it helps that i lost my cell phone @ *H-E-B* a few hours ago. so anyway, thanks kids. ill be back after a fashion. our bus departs in an hour.

Let me give you a case study and keep in mind that you can't change the dynamics of the case. So you have to go to two stores, the grocery store is on the right and the discount store is on left. Remember you have to go to both. Let's say you need to buy deodorant, which store will you buy your deodorant from? Again, you have to go to both. I've done this scenario many times.

MóTO: soooo . . . back in austin. however, my phone is lost. possibly @ *H-E-B* or in the depth's of maribel's car . . . or worse . . . her room. either way, if you need to reach me, try email. i lost it last week, so if you called, i cant call you back or have any way of knowing you called. but good news . . . i made it back safely. TM: yaaaay! longest week ever. no mas mexico MóTO: i know i totes missed you! JOH: this going in my book. MóTO: what is going in your book? i want rights . . . JOH: your update is going in my book. you can get a shout out. MF: my name is going in someone's book? yay my 15 min. of fame!

Reasons why Meli likes *Costco*: 1. *Costco* sells theme park food. Most notably, churros. 2. *Costco* introduced snack-sized foods into my childhood lunches. Before my mom discovered *Costco*, my pack lunches consisted of ziplox bags filled with potato chips. I felt embarassed because all the other kids had little name-brand bags of chips! And although mine were mostly Frito Lays, my peers couldn't tell from the clear plastics bags that they were in. Once my mom discovered snack purchases in bulk, I began to have appropriate snack-size foods included in my bagged lunches. 3. Buying bulk = helping out. When I was growing up, most of my aunts on my mother's side were struggling single mothers. My mom would always let my aunts know when she was planning on going to *Costco*. Allowing them to buy bulk was her way of helping them out. Whenever my mom ships big boxes to Guatemala, along with hand-me-down clothing, there are always *Costco* purchases. 4. *Costco* has rides! When I was younger, *Costco* had flat bed shopping carts. These were awesome! They were more dangerous than regular shopping carts because one slip of the foot meant you might get injured. Still, my dad let me sit on them. 5. *Costco* is a rite of passage. Part of becoming a semi-adult involved obtaining a *Costco* membership. My parents decided I should get my own card since I had moved away to go to college and finally had a place of my own. I was most excited when I got my picture taken! Me, a *Costco* member? Yessss! 6. *Costco* helps you find the perfect gift. Whenever my dad goes to Guatemala he buys chocolate bars in bulk. These he distributes among his many nieces and nephews. 7. Unlike other things in life, *Costco* has only disappointed me once. I remember discovering the sad reality that an underage card holder could not buy liquor even if a 21+ person was buying. Yes, *Costco* disappointed me that day.

MóTO: likes getting a morning coffee from cherrywood (when they arent being DBags), running into katie & wesley @ *Wheatsville Co-op*, buying a poetry book from half-priced books with maribel & the general enjoyable climate of a friday afternoon @ PDL. it keeps the madness self-contained. now if only my effing IPOD would do what i want. MJ: i snuck out of the office and am working on the patio at Bennu. It's freaking awesome outside right now! whatcha doing this weekend? MóTO: tomorrow . . . some fundraiser thing + some mikey time. sunday i have an engagement party to go to. tonight . . . open? drink later?

One thing that I do is tell myself how many things I need to remember, i.e. if I'm going to the grocery store I tell myself "I need to get four things at the grocery store," then as I'm wandering around the store, or before I get in line I ask myself, "How many things was I supposed to get? . . . Did I get all four things?" Also helps to remind me to *go* the grocery store, as in "I need to stop 2 places before I go home, the gas station and the grocery store," etc, etc.

I'm going to the grocery store today to stock up on wet cat and dog food. I don't care if it makes their poop stinky if it means I get many more years with them and they don't have to suffer through kidney failure and dialysis.

MóTO: i prefer andres . . . it's $5 at the fiesta market next to my house . . . i aint no fancy messican

JOH kissed MF en el *Fiesta*, ATX. Y le gustó.

The customers at the store have restricted not only where they shop for certain selections, but how they eat. One of the most restricted diets is that of a vegan.

MóTO: all i can do is stay brown until i die . . . (overheard @ *H-E-B* checkout counter) JOH: can't do nothing but MóTO: also, in honor of national coming out day, it is also very good to be queer. not just today. but every day. so many beautiful women in the world.

¿Cuántos de ustedes confiarían en el Otro, hoy en día?
Antes nomás gritaba por el CB, "Voy a la tienda y cuando
regrese vamos a tener un BBQ! ¿Alguien
quiere algo?" Y luego iba a comprar la comida.
Generalmente: unos bistecs o un par de libras de hamburguesa,
junto con una bolsa de papas y tal vez (los fines de semana)
una caja de cerveza. Y luego todos los traileros
ponían su parte como habíamos planeado. Ni una vez
me hicieron tranza. ¿Honestidad? Hell, yeah!
No más. ¡La camaradería ha desaparecido!

Soy uno de los mayores defensores de las checklists.

     Por ejemplo, si voy

al supermercado y necesito 30

    cosas, sin una lista,

puedo ser capaz de recordar 9

       de ellas, o con el uso de las categorizaciones

       de las cosas como las carnes,

verduras, etc, incluso 25

de las cosas, tal vez hasta 29,

pero si no tengo las 30,

       me siento ineficiente porque voy a tener

       que volver a la tienda.

Yo, literalmente, vivo por las checklists.

Wheatsville: A Dialogue

Huerta: Walking into this supermarket feels like a breath of fresh air.

Falcón: Why do you feel that way?

Huerta: I like how the manager greeted me personally with "Welcome to *Wheatsville.*"

Falcón: And do you feel welcomed?

Huerta: Well, sure, look at all the smiling faces and at how well lit this place is. There seems to be a pleasant attitude to this store.

Falcón: You described your pleasant feeling as a breath of fresh air. I want you to take a closer look at the entrance. What do you see above the automatic doors?

Huerta: Oh, a large fan.

Falcón: So do you think that this fan and its slight push of air on your face was part of why you felt that fresh breath?

Huerta: I suppose.

Falcón: But you were not aware of this when you entered the store and simply attributed the pleasantness to the manager's seeming hospitality.

Huerta: No, I was not aware of it.

Falcón: So do you agree that we're not always aware of what provokes our feelings and that we need to apply observation and thought in order to understand more fully the places we enter.

Huerta: I suppose. But I also felt the welcome feeling even before I walked into the store and was greeted by the manager and the big fan.

Falcón: How so?

Huerta: I guess it was the shaded outdoor area where those other customers were enjoying their meals. Seeing people seated out there made me feel invited, like this is a cool place to hang out at.

Falcón: Do you think those customers saw you before you saw them?

Huerta: I'm guessing they had a chance to see me first because from their seats they have a view of the whole parking lot.

Falcón: And is that view by design?

Huerta: It must be.

Falcón: For what purpose?

Huerta: So they can keep an eye on their vehicles. And I guess so they can keep an eye on anyone who enters the parking lot.

Falcón: So they have their eyes on us before we even get out of the vehicle. What do you think their eyes focus on?

Huerta: Well, no offence, but they were probably focusing on how beat-up your truck is.

Falcón: Well due to the high prices and lack of education on healthy food choices, low-income people of color do not find this store an economically feasible option. Most of the community cannot even enter the space. So yes, my old Chevrolet doesn't necessarily match the vehicles of the usual customers.

Huerta: And that means that we don't match the usual customers. That we don't belong.

Falcón: But if we don't belong. Then why did the manager personally greet us at the entrance? And why do we continue to receive smiling faces from people in the store.

Huerta: There must be something else behind the smiles and the welcomes.

Falcón: Consider a smiling face. Is it possible for a person to smile and still keep an eye on you?

Huerta: Yes.

Falcón: Then it would even be possible to hide an observing gaze behind a smiling face.

Huerta: Yes, so the manager could have personally greeted us not only because it's his job to be nice to the customer but also because it's his job to keep an eye on us.

Falcón: Yes, and let's take a second look at the manager, an "established insider." He's at a front circular counter. Why?

Huerta: That position allows him to monitor everyone who comes into the store as well as the line of cashiers behind him.

Falcón: Now that we have identified two checkpoints—the gaze of the customers seated outside and the manager's monitoring of everyone who enters the store—let's step a bit deeper into the store and see what we encounter. Do you see any store employees?

Huerta: I can't tell.

Falcón: And at other supermarkets how can you identify the employees?

Huerta: Well, they wear uniforms. For example, people that work at *H-E-B* wear a red polo.

Falcón: Yes, because they are required. But here at *Wheatsville* employees are not bound by any dress code. They often wear jeans and T-shirts, their hair is done to their preference, and visible tattoos are not uncommon. The only way to distinguish them as employees is by a small plastic name tag that most employees do not always wear.

Huerta: I guess the casual dress seems to fit with the pleasant attitude of the store. Maybe it could also be a way to promote trust between employees and customers. No uniform could be a way of communicating no formal authority.

Falcón: Yes, but remember that we have already agreed that there could be something else behind the seeming pleasantness of the store. So what other motive could there be to have *Wheatsville* employees look like everyday customers?

Huerta: If it's difficult to tell who is an employee and who is not, then we don't know who is part of the formal authority and who is not, who is watching us and who is not. Almost like a hidden camera.

Falcón: In what way? Say more.

Huerta: Well, when the camera is visible you are aware that you are being watched. When the camera is hidden you only get a sense that you are being watched.

Falcón: If it's hidden how do you know there is a hidden camera?

Huerta: Well I don't for sure. So then I assume that there is always the possibility of a hidden camera.

Falcón: What you are describing is called internalized surveillance. And in this store, the constant gaze of the hidden employees causes us to internalize the surveillance mechanism into an automated function.

Huerta: So it's not just that they are watching us, but that we are watching ourselves.

Falcón: Let's proceed to the checkout. Notice how when we arrive at the checkout counter, we are greeted once again by a smiling face. The counters are relatively small so that there is an intimate connection between the worker and the customer. The cashier is now required to ask, "Are you an owner of the co-op?" How does the question make you feel?

Huerta: Like I have to disclose something about myself. Almost like a confession.

Falcón: What you are describing is called the confessionary complex, the condition of an anxious self-disclosing citizen. It is a way for the public and private authority to gain consent for surveillance and social sorting.

Huerta: So I have to confess that I am not an owner. That I don't belong.

Falcón: Yes, and thus surveyed as a non-established insider. And imagine if you had to use food stamps. At *Wheatsville*, in order for this transaction to happen, you must confess that you are a welfare recipient to the cashier

Huerta: Really? That's not how other stores do it. Most stores allow for the customer to manually choose EBT as their method of payment.

Falcón: And what do you think of having to disclose this private Information?

Huerta: It seems like it's another way of keeping track of customers that maybe don't belong.

Falcón: This method is not only technological surveillance, but also a means to marginalize those who do not fit into the norms of the *Wheatsville* customer.

Huerta: I guess I don't feel so welcomed anymore.

Falcón: It's important to understand spaces and places by applying thoughtful analysis instead of simply relying on blind feelings.

Huerta: Well, let's go. I'm tired of being watched.

This dialogue is an adaptation of an undergraduate essay written by Maribel Falcón as a requirement for her Surveillance and Society class at UT Austin.

Las Aventuras de La Dos en Costcolandia

Este cuento se trata de dos fascinaciones: 1. mi fascinación con La Dos 2. la fascinación de La Dos con el Costco. I should say "nuestra fascinación" porque somos dos los que estamos fascinados con La Dos: 1. El Pie Derecho 2. El Pie Izquierdo. El Pie Izquierdo y El Pie Derecho —ese soy yo— walk to the El Cerrito Costco because we have heard that La Dos lives in one of the aisles. We look for her in aisle #2, but La Dos is not there. We ask one of the stockboys where we could find her, but he tells us a joke instead.

"What do you call los enamorados de La Dos?"

"¿Qué?"

"¡Los PerdiDOS!"

The stockboy laughs uncontrollably, and as we walk away he says, "One day when you have forgotten it you will hear the joke for a second time, but this time from La Dos, and I promise you will feel like you're dying from the laughter."

Just outside of aisle #2, we encounter a second stockboy, and he points and gives us directions. "1. you want to go ➜. 2. you want to go ←." El Pie Izquierdo goes ←, and I—El Pie Derecho—go ➜.

Encontramos a La Dos lying in the makeshift aisle between the wine bottles and the breakfast breads. She greets us with a huge smile :D .

"¿Por qué tan feliz?" preguntamos.

"Because I'm eating the second saddest fruit. May I interest you in some canned peaches?"

"Do you feel sad when you eat the second happiest fruit?"

"Of course not. The second happiest fruit is pineapples, and they hold sunshine."

As we enjoy our canned peaches, we inform La Dos that we are interested in writing a book about her experiences called *Las Aventuras de La Dos en Costcolandia*. She flashes a huge smile :D. "We should start with some basic information you should know about me," says La Dos and gestures to El Pie Izquierdo that he should record what she says in our notebook. La Dos begins, "I'm an extrovert on the inside. I'm trained as an urban planner, but I'm bad with directions. I put on my pants two legs at a time. I have two friends named Claudia, but I refer to each Claudia as Claudia #1."

I turn to El Pie Izquierdo and say, "Son dos Claudias."

El Pie Izquierdo writes it down and below that he adds, "Solo hay una Dos."

And La Dos continues, "I have been in love only once, pero de dos personas. O tal vez me enamoré dos veces pero solo de una persona. I met him here at Costco. He still works as a stock-boy in aisle #2 and likes to tell jokes about me."

El Pie Izquierdo looks at me to suggest that this would be a good time to tell La Dos what we came to tell her. In reality we have come to Costco to declare our fascination. "Dos, tengo dos cosas que decirte: 1. me fascinas. 2. me fascinas." Pero tenemos un problema de dos porque lo pensamos dos veces y al fin decimos dos nadas.

La Dos starts up with a huge smile :D because she remembers it is time for free samples. She grabs both of us by the arm and guides us to what she calls "bite-size wonder." And it is wonderful. We eat gelato, hummus, crackers, chocolates and wings, and we drink it all down with cappucino and water. La Dos laughs at El Pie Izquierdo y El Pie Derecho —ese soy yo—

when the gelato server scolds us because we try to grab a second sample.

Then La Dos sees a huge Costco cart and runs to it. We follow behind. One Costco cart is as big as two regular grocery carts, and they come equipped to accommodate two babies with two legs each. La Dos says, "May I interest you in a ride." El Pie Izquierdo and I sit down and let our legs dangle. This makes La Dos smile :D. La Dos pushes the cart and us to the fridge, which, as she claims, is big enough to walk around in.

"You should go inside to get me a case of milk and see for yourself how huge the fridge is," La Dos says.

When El Pie Izquierdo and I step into the fridge, La Dos closes the glass door on us. We look back to see her huge smile :D. El Pie Izquierdo and I act afraid until she lets us out. When we hand her a case of milk, La Dos says, "See. In one case, you get two gallons of milk. Costco believes everyone should have a friend to share milk with. You two should take this one home."

El Pie Izquierdo whispers to me that we are running out of time and that we should tell La Dos exactly what we came to tell her. La Dos wants to know what we are whispering about. We want to say, "Dos, tengo dos cosas que decirte. 1. quiero sentir la singularidad de la Dos. 2. quiero sentir la singularidad de La Dos." Pero lo único que nos sale son dos silencios. We could have enjoyed two glorious joys for the price of one. La Dos breaks los dos silencios with her beautiful smile :D. "Tengo dos cosas que darles: 1. My recipe for black bean patties. 2. My recipe for white bean patties."

"Dos, why do you love Costco so much?" we ask her.

"Because bulk is beautiful," she says.

And as she guides us through the Costco aisles looking for ingredients, El Pie Izquierdo y yo, El Pie Derecho, find ourselves alone in ailse #2 not knowing when La Dos had left us. The stockboy, the one who was loved twice by La Dos, is still there.

"May I interest you in a piece of Tres Leches cake?"

El Pie Izquierdo y El Pie Derecho, ese so yo, take one piece and split it in half. El Pie Izquierdo takes 1 ½ and I take 1 ½.

"I thought eating Tres Leches cake would help me move beyond La Dos," the stockboy says.

"But it tastes like the second saddest cake," we say, El Pie Izquierdo y El Pie Derecho.

"Do you know why they call her La Dos?"

"¿Por qué?" preguntamos.

"Porque tiene dos ojos costcoltecos."

Terminaremos

nuestro viaje de compras con una prueba de sabor

de algunos

de los alimentos en nuestra lista de supermercado.

Clasifique

los alimentos que compró por alimentos saludables

y los alimentos

chatarra. Va a hacer dos columnas en su diario,

una por una

alimentación sana y una por la comida chatarra.

Va a poner

cada elemento que se encuentra en su receta bajo el título

correcto,

saludable o no deseado. Vamos a tratar una variedad

de frutas y

vegetales. Usted y su compañero de equipo, van

a tocar, oler,

probar y escuchar cómo suenan estos alimentos cuando

los mastican

o cortan. Usted tendrá la oportunidad de probar cada uno

de los alimentos

y escribir en su diario sobre la experiencia. Dibuje o use

un corte

de imagen para representar cada alimento que se ordena.

Debe elegir

al menos 2 de sus alimentos favoritos de la prueba de sabor

y dibujar

esos en su diario, así como para escribir acerca de por qué

le gustaban.

Tootsie va
a la tienda.
La comida ya
se le acabó
y salió
. . . corriendo

American Copia

Today I'm going to the store with all the lovely possibilities of food.

Purgatory—that's what María calls our existence when we live in the Extended Stay in Emeryville and shop for groceries at *Pac & Save*. It is January of 2006. María and I have just driven a U-haul with all of our belongings from El Paso, Texas, to the San Francisco Bay Area. We don't yet have an apartment, so we're staying at the Extended Stay for two and a half weeks. Up and down the aisles of the *Pac & Save*, María and I, hand-in-hand, walk by, around and through shadows. The whole produce section before us. Those who love us pray for us.

On Day 253 of 1987 Alien # A090891109 and his little brother Alien # A090891110 will go to Supermercado #3 with their mother Alien # A090891108. And this is poetry.

My mother sends my younger brother Tomás to the *Foodarama* on South Post Oak, and I ask him if I can go with him. I'm looking for an opportunity to have a talk with him so I can apologize. I want to say that I'm sorry for not putting up a fight when that hand snatched the gold chain with the gold crucifix from my neck as I was walking the halls of Westbury High. I want to tell him that I know that's one of the few connections he had with our father. But I don't say anything, only offer to help when he grabs two cases of sodas in each hand.

Lately, I'm trying to plan my week's menu in advance. That way, I only have to go to the grocery store a couple times a week, saving gas and time (and me the headache of lugging two kids to the store).

Most little kids love public transportation and again this can require some schlepping, but it can make going to the grocery store a real adventure.

La tanda is an immigrant community phenomenon that may need some explanation. A group of individuals sign up and come to an agreement that they will each place, let's say, $200 into a pot. This is done each month until each of the members gets a share of the pot. This system should not be confused with a pyramid scheme. La tanda provides immigrants who may not have access to bank accounts a means of saving money. When someone buys a new living room set or goes on a vacation, you can guess that they must have just received la tanda. So my Tía Alma was especially upset that night when she went to *Foodarama* to buy groceries for the week and accidentally left her purse in the car, in plain view. While pushing a cart down the aisles, she remembered her purse and ran out into the parking lot. It was too late. Her window laid in shattered pieces on the ground. The purse was gone. She went inside to ask the workers, especially those who corral the grocery carts, whether they had seen anything. They said no, but she didn't believe them. She could cancel her credit cards, but she had not yet delivered the $1,500 she had recently collected for this month's tanda. Later, she received a call from *Foodarama* saying that they had found her purse. She asked if anything was in the purse. Tía Alma never went back to *Foodarama.*

I never announce when I'm going to the grocery store.

María and I are going to the *Safeway* on Grand in her new vehicle. She has bought a white Toyota Rav4 and has named it "Nelson," after George Washington's white horse. The new vehicle does have an advantage over our old VW Bug. It comes equipped with a rack and a net where we can place groceries, especially those items that might shift during the drive home and fall out. But I miss our old car, The Beast. It was raffled off in a benefit for María's Puente Students. A young female student ended up with the car. Sometimes when I spot a yellow VW Bug on the road, I wonder if it's The Beast and whether it's headed to the grocery store.

After I finished reading from a draft of *American Copia* at the Percolator in El Paso, Texas, an international engineering graduate student at UTEP handed me the following note, "The people in my country were dying on the streets, and I, here, half of a world far from home, was going to the grocery store, every day! (I am from Iran. The cruel government killed and turned protesters who thought the election was a fraud in the last couple of months in Iran. I was crying and living in a nightmare, every day of my life those days. But as you said, Life should go on . . . as we go on to the grocery store). Sincerely—Nila."

This little javi went to market; this little javi stayed at home; this little javi had roast beef; this little javi had none; and this little javi went wee wee wee all the way home.

With two email accounts—and a fairly active volume of emails at work which need to be responded to immediately, I find that most of my employed friends are too busy for the "I'm going to the grocery store now" banter.

I often wonder if I would have grown up thin had my family stayed and bought groceries in Mexico. The day we crossed the river my seven-year-old body had not an ounce of fat on it. It didn't take long before I transformed into a pudgy little bastard. When we returned to Nuevo Laredo eight years later, one of my uncles commented on my size by grabbing my belly and my little brother's belly and saying, "Y dicen que hay crisis en los Estados Unidos." What are the reasons why my little brother and I gained weight? It could be a Houston thing. *Men's Fitness* magazine ranked Houston at the top of "America's Fattest Cities" for three straight years, 2001, 2002, 2003, and suggested the following reason: "Given the region's climate (hot and humid), air quality (abysmal) and relative lack of outdoor recreation, staying active presents a Texas-style challenge." It could be a poverty thing. Many studies have found a relationship between poverty and obesity.

María and I now have a membership card for *Safeway*, which means we can benefit from a lot of great deals. After we load our groceries into Nelson, I read the statement of our savings on the receipt in percentages and dollars. We usually save about 20 to 30 dollars. That I read the savings somehow reassures María.

My poet friend Craig Santos Pérez says that I need to stop going to the grocery store or I will never finish my copia. That same day I go to the supermarket and buy myself a can of Spam.

I'm going to the grocery store so I can get that prime parking space and not have to wait in line. Plus, my list isn't too long so I'll be in and out in a jiffy.

Today I will go to the grocery store and buy a loaf of bread. Bread always brings to mind this quote by De Crèvecoeur, "His country is now that which gives him land, bread, protection and consequence; *Ubi panis ibi patria*, is the motto of all emigrants." De Crèvecoeur, a French immigrant, wrote a collection of epistolary essays about American life entitled *Letters from an American Farmer.* The quoted passage appears in the letter, "What is an American?" I find it interesting that in his attempt to answer this question Crèvecoeur focuses his discussion on immigrants. The immigrant does not look at the mythic foundation of nations; the immigrant is a pragmatic individual. That immigrant motto, I believe, is echoed in Ramón "Tianguis" Pérez's *Diario de un Mojado*. Pérez speaks of "la lógica del mojado": "Si no le es favorable en un lugar, tal vez será mejor en otro." I had this discussion in mind when I wrote the poem, "Sobre el pan," which appears in my book *Some Clarifications*. Here I provide a translation:

> Don't say that bread
>
> is a cushion. Much less
> a pillow. And don't
>
> you dare say that it is
> a cloud. Bread is bread.
>
> Our stomachs
> don't have a right to more.

Quote. Strange that honey/ can't be got without hard money. End Quote. Keats, again.

I'm going to the grocery store tomorrow, too, so I'll be doing lots of label reading. If I can't pronounce it I don't buy it. I don't buy 95% of the food at a normal grocery store, and that number is getting smaller and smaller as I find healthier markets/farms to buy food from. Meat aisle, fish, veggies, fruit and I'm out of there. These days I'm getting less and less meat from there.

I want to produce a supermarket dating show for Latin@s. The contestants would go to the grocery store on their first date and buy ingredients to cook a dinner together. The show, I tell María, could be called *A Pinch o' Love*. She suggests I should call it *A Pinche Love*.

Food stamps are an entitlement program with eligibility guidelines set by Congress and the federal government paying for benefits while states pay most administrative costs. Eligibility is determined by a complex formula, but basically recipients must have few assets and incomes below 130% of the poverty line, or less than $27,560 for a family of four.

On January 5, 2008, I write a bio for the *Achiote Seeds* Winter 2008 issue, in which nine pages of *American Copia*—or as I call it, "my grocery store poem"—are to be published. I send the bio to Craig Santos Pérez, poet and cofounder/editor with Jenn Reimer of Achiote Press. The bio reads, "Javier Huerta is the author of *Some Clarifications y otros poemas* (Arte Público 2007), which received the 31st (2005) Chicano/Latino Literary Prize from UC Irvine. Currently he is a graduate student in the English Department at UC Berkeley. He lives in Oakland with the novelist and painter, María, who is waiting for him to finish writing this bio so they can go to the grocery store."

Hopefully there won't be guys at the supermarket deli counter asking me to teach them english, or taxi bike drivers asking if I want them to drive my stuff home, or random guys in the street hissing at me.

"Javi, grab the bags and run to the car," my Tía Pera says. I grab the bags and pretend to start running. My cousin Cynthia says, "Don't do it. I'll chase after and get you. I'm not scared of you." Tía Pera and I go to the *Fiesta* on Bellaire and Hillcroft, partly because she needs some items but mostly because we wanted to drop in on my little cousin Cynthia, who is working as a cashier. Cynthia works nights because she is still in high school. She is working because she had a baby at the young age of 15. Earlier during lunch she tells me how a couple of nights ago, she ran after someone who hadn't paid. She knew that loss would come out of her pay. She understands the value of a dollar. The manager admonished her and told her not to chase anyone like that because it could put her in danger. We, my aunt and I, joke about this while she's ringing up our items. Before we go, my Tía asks her why she parked her truck so far from the front doors. Since Cynthia gets off work at midnight, my Tía is concerned for her safety. My Tía is disabled, so she has parked the other truck in the handicap space close to the doors. She tells Cynthia that she's going to switch trucks with her so she can have the one parked closer to the door. After we move our stuff from one truck to the other, I run in and hand the keys to my little cousin Cynthia, who is all grown up.

I get dressed everyday with the thoughts of "I'm going somewhere important today" so I always try to look my best, even if I'm going to the grocery store.

6 ½ smoke alarms later, María says, never again para nada. For 2007 María and I order a Thanksgiving dinner from *Whole Foods*. When we pick it up we expect the dinner to be already cooked. But what they give us is a box with a frozen turkey, frozen green beans, frozen mashed potatoes and frozen other stuff. The box does come with instructions. María and I decide to proceed.

I'm going to the grocery store this afternoon. Alvis and I are going to have some fun in the backyard! (If Lavie doesn't catch us!)

You're not overweight, Javier! But the connection between poverty and obesity, or alternately, in much of the developing world, poverty and plain old starvation, is a very real one. You probably already know this book, but Raj Patel's *Stuffed and Starved* is excellent on this point.

I never refuse seconds. You can tell this by looking at me. Since I don't make a habit of stepping on the scale, I really can't say in precise numbers how overweight I am, but I can say that the label *gordo* would not be inappropriate. Do I have a weight problem? No, because María, my partner, the woman I love, does not seem to mind. She actually likes that she has difficulty wrapping her arms all the way around me. She even likes to pull up my shirt and bite on my belly. I don't get it either. But if it works for her, it works for me. All of this is just to say that I would make an awful hunger artist.

I'm going to the grocery store to get some brownschweiger . . . I've never figured out how to spell it, and think I may spell it different each time I try.

The most crucial event in history—after the creation of borders and the invention of poetry—is Margarita Gómez going to the supermarket.

On May 2, 2009, María and I walk into *Mi Pueblo Food Center* in East Oakland to buy ingredients to cook chile rellenos. It is her birthday and chile rellenos is her favorite Mexican dish. I ask my mother for her recipe. As soon as I walk in, the hypermexican colores and olores assault my senses. Mi Pueblo. Mi Pueblo. Mi Pueblo. I experience authentic nostalgia inspired by the inauthentic feeling of home created by a Mexican supermarket. And all I could do was tremble. When I recover María and I start selecting the ingredients on my mother's recipe for chile rellenos: chiles, aceite, huevos, harina, tomates, cebolla, consomé de carne, queso. We don't know what type of cheese to get so I phone my mother in Tejas. She says to use queso fresco. Then knowing that it was a week before Mother's Day, I ask her, "¿Qué le dio Batman a su mamá para el Día de las Madres?" She responds, "¿Qué, mijo?" The punchline: "¡una batidora!" Mi amá laughed hysterically. María did not understand the laughter, and I resented her for it. María, perdóname. This is the last time María and I would go to the grocery store together.

Is anybody else tired of hearing produce trucks illegally honking their horns all day long everyday? Not to mention parking in the middle of the street and encouraging loitering. Please respond back if you are fed up with these guys, I want to get a simple petition together to send to the police station and to our city council representative. If you don't actually hear these trucks you might still want to help get rid of them because it would clean up the area and raise everybody's property values. Thanks for your help.

María: The awful truth is that there are times when I can't be the clown. I am held down by deep sadness. I assume no one wants to be near me because if I can't smile and laugh, how can they? I feel better in the mornings. I sometimes think that it wasn't me who sobbed for an hour about the mindless couple who discussed their need for crackers and ketchup in the grocery store line.

Two months after my grandmother passed away, I visit mi Tía Pera, and she tells me a story about her "mita," her term of endearment for my abuelita chole. My grandmother was eagerly anticipating the grand opening of the new dollar store in the neighborhood. She called her friend Lupe, who came to pick her up, and they waited along with many others for the doors to open. Mi abuelita already had a list of items that she wanted to buy. When they opened the doors, my grandmother and her friend and everyone else charged in. The fumes of a chemical they had used to clean/paint overwhelmed them. My 80-something-year-old grandmother passed out. The paramedics came and took many of the customers to the emergency room to get treated. Mi Tía received a call informing her of the emergency, and she rushed to find my grandmother. When she got there everything was fine, but my grandmother was ecstatic to see her youngest daughter. My grandmother said that she was scared because she didn't know where the paramedics were taking them. Tía Pera laughs all through the telling of the story. When I get ready to leave, she tells me, "Don't forget to say goodbye to your abuelita." She has kept an altar in my grandmother's room with candles and a framed picture. I go looking for mi abuelita chole in her old room.

All I have for you right now is that one time at *Fiesta* I got a canadian coin instead of a quarter, and I asked if you thought people ever got pesos in Canada. And you said, "I wish one of us were smart enough to really write about that." But that's just a funny memory.

But if I'm going to the grocery store that is three miles away, it's pretty stupid to punch this in my GPS.

Little Meli did not pee in her pants at *Ralph's*. She did not go to *Ralph's* with her mother after she picked her up from school. She did not tell her mother that she needed to use the restroom, and her mother did not tell her to just hold it because she wasn't going to take long. Little Meli did not pee in her pants at *Ralph's*. She did not cry after she did not pee in her pants at *Ralph's*. Her mother did not make her walk around *Ralph's* with wet pink sweatpants. She did not walk around *Ralph's* with wet pink sweatpants. She did not think about kids at school who did not pee in their pants. She did not think about how the school kids did not laugh at the kids who did not pee in their pants. She did not say that she did not want to ever be like those kids who did not pee in their pants. She did not say that she did not want to ever be like those kids who did not pee in their pants and did not get laughed at. Not So Little Meli does not make sure to go peepee before she leaves any place. Not So Little Meli does not make sure to go peepee before she leaves any place whether she has to pee or not pee. Not So Little Meli does not make fun of Little Meli , "To pee or not to pee—that is not the question." Not So Little Meli does not need to talk about the time when Little Meli did not pee in her pants at *Ralph's*.

You might consider announcing the day before you do your grocery shopping that tomorrow's shopping day. If anyone needs anything, they should get it on the list now.

As a share of the national population, food stamp use was highest in 1994, after several years of poor economic growth, with an average of 27.5 million recipients per month from a lower total of residents. The numbers plummeted in the late 1990s as the economy grew and legal immigrants and certain others were excluded. But access by legal immigrants has been partly restored, and in the current decade, the federal and state governments have used advertising and other measures to inform people of their eligibility and have often simplified application procedures.

There's a supermarket down the street from Lake Merritt. It is close enough so that the homeless woman asking for change in front of the store can see the lights that crown the lake at night. I hope you remember it fondly. (I say "you," but you know this "you" refers to you, María.) I used to sneak up behind you to steal a grope or two as you selected fruit for the week. Then you'd send me to get the fancy potatoes. And I'd say that our finances can't be that bad if we can afford not to get the big bag of russet potatoes. Though the name has changed, the supermarket is still there. So is the lake and its crown of lights. So is the night. The woman still asks for change and is still homeless. But couples no longer shop there. Couples no longer enter this supermarket that is down the street from Lake Merritt.

Agradecimientos

I am indebted first and foremost to María P. Tuttle. Not only because in our five-year relationship we went to the grocery store together an abundant number of times but also because she was the first to suggest that *American Copia* should be a book-length project. * I'm also grateful for Alma Granado and the time she spent with me in the Summer and Fall of 2009. In my time of crisis Alma guided me to the grocery store and to the writing of this book. * Gracias, Melissa. I hope you have as much fun reading this work as I had writing it. * I'm indebted to Craig Santos Pérez and Jennifer Reimer, co/editors of Achiote Press, for soliciting and publishing the first 11 pages of *American Copia*. * Thanks also to Paul Martínez Pompa for soliciting and publishing 2 pages of "La Pouty" excerpts in *Ariel*. * Gracias a León Salvatierra and the editors of El Mercado for publishing "Anonimo" * Thanks to my friends and colleagues in The Xican@ Culture Working Group (XWG), an interdisciplinary group of UC Berkeley graduate students interested in engaging with Chicana/o cultural production (art, music, literature, film, dissertations, teatro, activism and poetry). In Spring 2009 the core members of XWG included Alejandro, Alma, Gabriela, Javier, Jorge, Marisol, Robert and Sara. * Thank you to the Victorian Reading Group/Supper Club, a group of Berkeley grad students in preparation for qualifying exams who came together every other week to discuss Victorian Literature and enjoy wonderful food. This group included Monica, Gina, Catherine, Ruth, Javier, Ben, John, Matt * Thanks also to all my friends who contributed to this book, Jill, Cecilia, Melissa, Monica, Jasper, Tia, Lili, Rich, Reb, Jenn, Nila, Adilene, Maribel, Julie * Gracias a León, mi broder de otra moder, for allowing me to include his supermarket experiences * Thanks to Mónica Teresa Ortiz for being brutally honest when she read earlier drafts of *American Copia* * Thank you to poets Oscar Bermeo and Barbara Jane Reyes for believing in this project from the beginning * Gracias a mis dos familias: Los Gómez y Los Huerta * Gracias a mi madre, Margarita Gómez, por ir a la tienda a comprar mandado para nosotros. And thanks to anyone who has ever gone to the grocery store with me.

Also by Javier O. Huerta

Some Clarifications y otros poemas